FALL FANTASIES
by

JUNE ZINKGRAF
and
TONI BAUMAN

illustrated by

June Zinkgraf

Toni Bauman

Judi Myhal

Copyright © Good Apple, Inc. 1980

ISBN 0-916456-61-7
Printing 123456789

GOOD APPLE
BOX 299
CARTHAGE, IL 62321

Dedicated to

June...

who planned, gathered, arranged, ordered and nestled
skybound arcs of color and light
and built for each child
a rainbow
no illusion or mirage--
real rounds of color
raised by weaving the practical notions of 2 plus 2
and the short sound of "a"
with the stretch and joy of bubble gum
My salute and thanks to you, Rainbow Builder
for the memories and dreams for children
and me

Toni

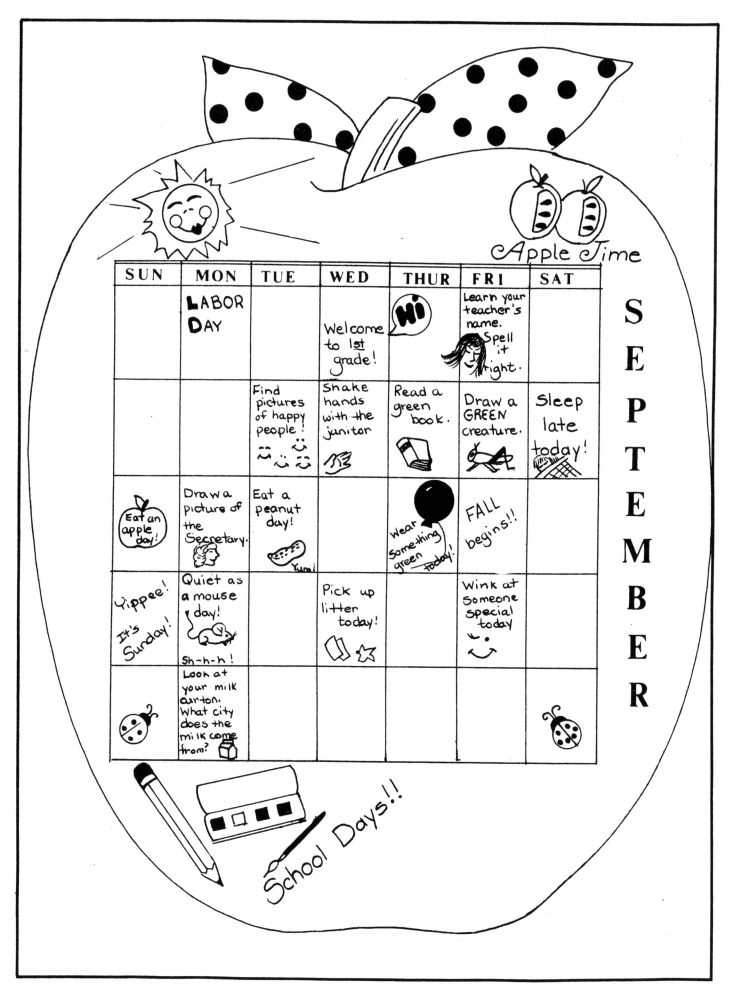

Apple Time

SUN	MON	TUE	WED	THUR	FRI	SAT
	LABOR DAY		Welcome to 1st grade!	Hi	Learn your teacher's name. Spell it right.	
		Find pictures of happy people!	Shake hands with the janitor	Read a green book.	Draw a GREEN creature.	Sleep late today!
Eat an apple day!	Draw a picture of the Secretary.	Eat a peanut day!		Wear something green today!	FALL begins!!	
Yippee! It's Sunday!	Quiet as a mouse day! Sh-h-h!		Pick up litter today!		Wink at someone special today	
	Look at your milk carton. What city does the milk come from?					

S E P T E M B E R

School Days!!

The kids are a little green but willing to try
With some good planning you're- - -

Off To...

A Hoppy Start!

Start with a topic that has a little jump to it and you'll capture the attention and motivate all the children in your room.....even the boys. Find a real frog, make some cutouts of its shadow and you will be off ....to a hoppy start!

WELCOME TO OUR PAD!

Begin by decorating the door to your classroom. Cut a L-A-R-G-E lily pad from green paper. Add the letters stating the theme, "Welcome to OUR Pad." Make a paper frog for each student. Print his/her name on it and stick it to the lily pad. Be sure to make a few extra blank frogs just in case a new student or two arrives without advance notice.

FIRST DAY FROG FUN

The first day of school can be very long unless you plan interesting activities. Try the "Frog Factor" worksheet found on the next page. Students should read each sentence. Wherever the word "ribbit" is found, students must insert the word which will correctly fill the blank. All sentences should have to do with the beginning of school.

A good second activity is "Leap Frog and Friends," also found on the next page. Students begin by filling their blank bingo sheet with autographs of the students in the class. One signature goes in each square. As you read names of the students, the students try to bingo. When the game is over, everyone will have a list of who is in the class.

THE FROG FACTOR

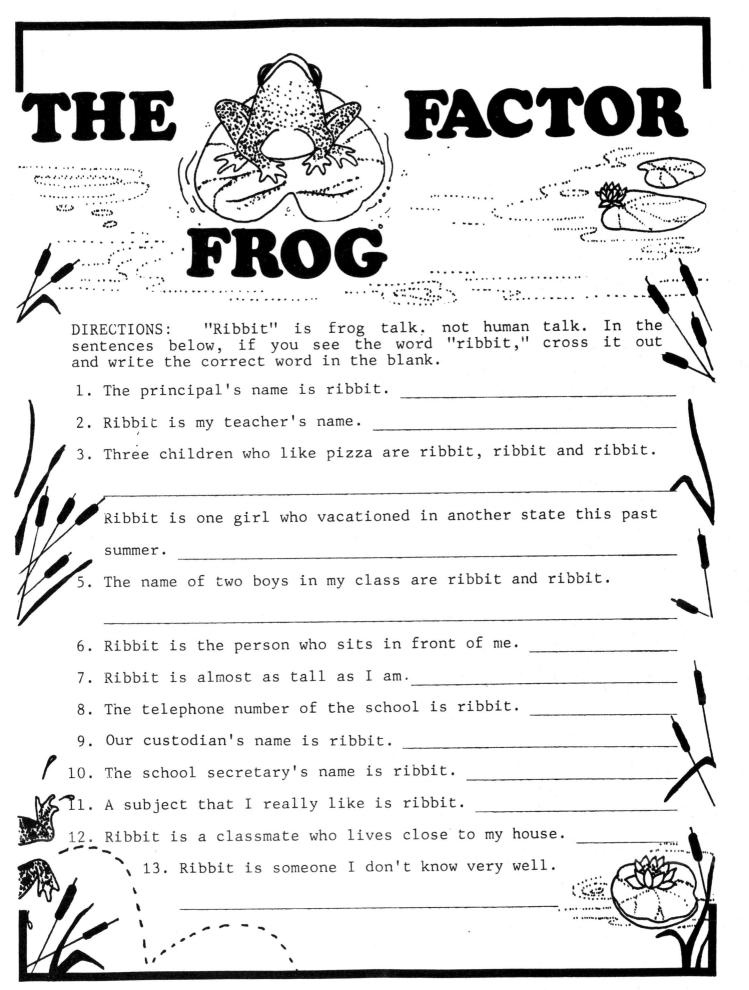

DIRECTIONS: "Ribbit" is frog talk, not human talk. In the sentences below, if you see the word "ribbit," cross it out and write the correct word in the blank.

1. The principal's name is ribbit. _____

2. Ribbit is my teacher's name. _____

3. Three children who like pizza are ribbit, ribbit and ribbit.

_____

Ribbit is one girl who vacationed in another state this past

summer. _____

5. The name of two boys in my class are ribbit and ribbit.

_____

6. Ribbit is the person who sits in front of me. _____

7. Ribbit is almost as tall as I am. _____

8. The telephone number of the school is ribbit. _____

9. Our custodian's name is ribbit. _____

10. The school secretary's name is ribbit. _____

11. A subject that I really like is ribbit. _____

12. Ribbit is a classmate who lives close to my house. _____

13. Ribbit is someone I don't know very well.

_____

HOPPY PATTERNS

Pattern

Pattern

Use the patterns on this page to make name tags for your students. Use them on lockers, desks, or to label anything that belongs to students. Use a variety of poses so all are not the same.

To make the frogs, cut the shapes from green tagboard or poster-board. Outline with black marker Add details with black or a dark green marker. Cut and laminate.

Pattern

Pattern

Pattern

LEAP FROG & FRIENDS

free

DIRECTIONS: Get the autograph of twenty people in your classroom. One autograph for each square. Now you are ready to play the game. The game will be played just like bingo!

DIRECTIONS: On the short lines below, write the letters of your
name in order. Warning! There may not be room for them all. Then,
on each longer line, write a phrase beginning with the letter on
the short line. Each phrase should tell something about you. It
might describe what you look like, what you eat, or something you
do. Read the whole thing when you finish. It will sound like a poem.

_____   _____

_____   _____

_____   _____

_____   _____

_____   _____

_____   _____

_____   _____

_____   _____

NOTES ON A NAME
a first week of school activity

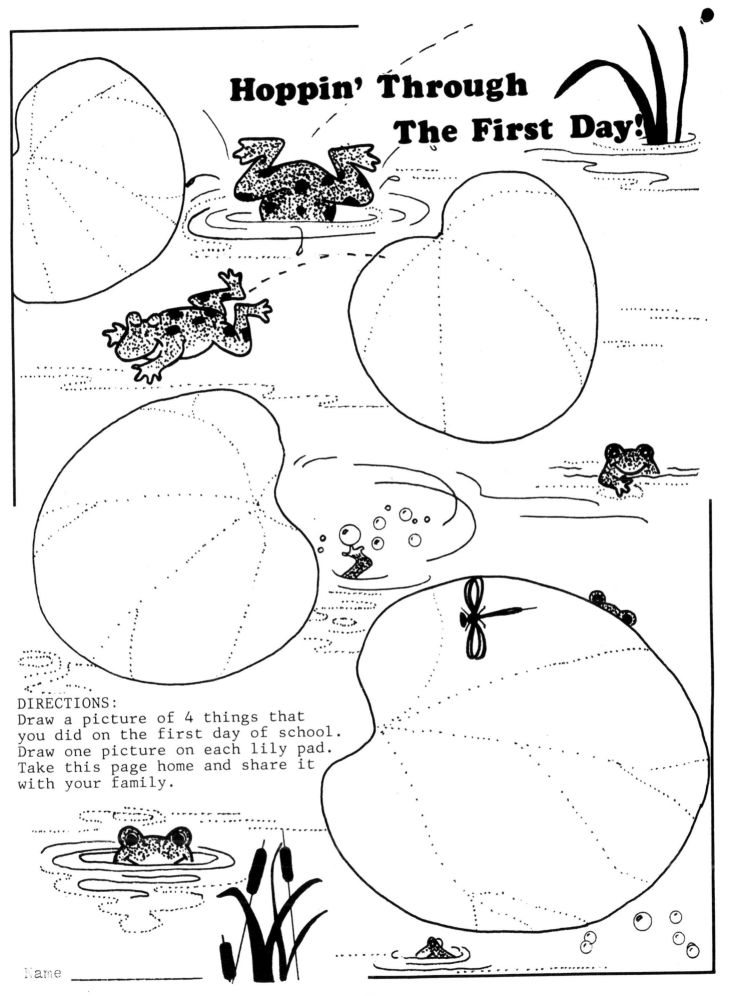

Hoppin' Through The First Day!

DIRECTIONS:
Draw a picture of 4 things that you did on the first day of school. Draw one picture on each lily pad. Take this page home and share it with your family.

Name _____

Froghouses
AND OTHER PROJECTS

Provide a collection of library books about frogs for your students to enjoy and use as reference material. The books can be placed in a corner of the room that has been decorated to look like a swamp. Place a jar of cattails and a terrarium in the area. A small green rug will also look nice.

NOTE: Not all of the books need to be reference books. Some can simply be books to read and enjoy. Pictures and filmstrips can also be included.

Using your swamp corner library, have children select one of the following projects. Consider having the children work in pairs to develop a spirit of cooperation as well as the science skills.

Project A: Use the books to determine all the elements necessary for a frog's environment. Design a home using an aquarium or an empty box. Use scrap paper or collage materials for details. Remember there are many kinds of frogs so label your froghouse properly.

Project B: Use a roll of shelf paper. Divide it into sections. Illustrate each stage of the development of a frog. Check the resource books for details and accuracy of the drawing.

Project C: Prepare a brief talk and explain to the class why a frog's skin must remain wet.

Project D. Make a Mini-book. Write one fact you learned about frogs on each page. Illustrate each fact. Make thumbprint frogs for your illustrations.

Project E: Make a Mini-dictionary. Read the books and find the meaning of the following words: amphibian, tadpoles, lungs, warm-blooded, cold-blooded, moist, algae, hibernate, protective coloration, and leopard frog.

Project F: Divide a large sheet of paper in half. On one half, draw a frog. On the other half, draw a toad. List the differences between the two similar creatures.

HOP TO IT!
- - - -a little frog fun!

FOSTER FROG

Find a foster frog! If you have a small friend who likes to scout the ponds for such creatures, you're in luck. Once the word is out that you're looking for a frog, it shouldn't take long for a volunteer to appear. Keep your frog in a box that will allow room for the frog to be wet as well as provide a place to be out of the water. Frogs will eat only live bugs, but can be tricked by hamburger bits or dead creatures dangled on a string. Place paper lily pads around the outside of your froghouse. Have students write words which they think describe the frog on the paper pads. Have a frog-naming contest. Pick the most original name. Have children estimate how long the frog is. Measure and find out. Measure each part of the frog. Which is longer, his back legs or front legs? Why?

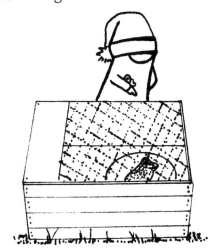

FROG FACTS

A few frog facts will help you stay in the know about the hoppy creatures. Frogs nestle in the mud in the winter and hibernate. Tree frogs with webbed and sticky feet are called spring peepers. A frog breathes through his lungs when on land and through pores in his skin when in the water. If the pores dry out, they close and the frog will die. A frog sheds his skin often. He eats the old skin. Throughout the world there are about 2000 kinds of frogs. Most are green, but not all are. All have wet skin. Frogs can leap twenty times their body length. Frogs do not blink. They rest by shutting their eyes halfway. They can still see through their eyelid which comes from below the eye.

FROGS 'N FICTION

Begin NOW, at the beginning of the year, to use good children's literature in your classroom as a regular part of the curriculum. As you organize any unit of study, select appropriate literature to correlate with the subject matter. Below are listed some good examples of frog fiction and follow-up activities for students. Check with your librarian for additional titles.

A Boy A Dog And A Friend (1967), Frog Where Are You ? (1973), Frog On His Own (1973), and One Frog Too Many, (1975) are four super frog books written by Mercer Mayer and published by Dial Press of New York.

Each is a delightful WORDLESS story which can be used by students regardless of their reading ability. The books are available in paperback. Consider buying two copies of each and taking them apart and hanging the pages on a bulletin board for students to see. Let children know that you want them to tell you what the story is by Friday. Or you may want students to write one sentence for each page. Using an opaque projector, project the pages onto a wall and talk about what is happening. There are excellent opportunities for language development and pre-reading comprehension.

Because of their special friendship, the Frog and Toad stories are naturals for the opening of school. They are written by Arnold Lobel and published by Harper Row, New York. The frog and toad are featured in various incidents in Frog And Toad Are Friends, Frog, and Toad Together, and Frog and Toad All Year. Told at the end of a busy day, the stories are a natural with an ice cream treat. The story "The Garden" in Frog And Toad Together is a delightful one for any age. Help your children remember good stories by sharing token souvenirs with them. For this story, give each child a small packet of seeds to plant in a garden.

Other good frog stories include The Strange Story Of The Frog Who Became a Prince, Horwitz, Delacorte Press, 1971, His Majesty, The Frog, Roth, Morrow Jr. Books, 1971 and The Old Bullfrog, Freschet, Scribner's and Sons, New York 1968.

" In summer dusk

he croaks

like jokes

played on a cello ..."

.....From A CHILD''S BEASTIARY
J. Gardner,
Alfred Knopf
New York, 1977

Don't fail to jump at the chance to share simple but good poetry with children. "Frog" from A Child's Bestiary, is an excellent beginning. Your library will have a copy of Arbuthnot's Anthology of Children's Literature, Houghton Mifflin, 1970. Find Conrad Aiken's poem "The Frog" in it and share with your students. Read it to the students and have them write parts and illustrate the parts on lily pad shaped paper.

gunk,

gunk,

went the little green frog.....

Review some of your favorite children's songs to add to the first week of school frog study. Have students make a frog puppet from a paper plate to use to sing-a-long with a frog song. Of course, don't forget the world famous KERMIT. If you do, Miss Piggy might get huffy.

......Froggie went a courtin'.......

How do you make a frog stew? (keep him waiting for 3 hours!)

What's white on the outside, green on the inside and hops? (a frog sandwich!)

Croaks & Riddles

There is nothing like a riddle to make children giggle with delight. Begin by cutting lily pad-shaped lift-up sheets. Fold the paper and cut a double image leaving the top, bottom or side uncut. Write the riddle on the outside of the lily pad and the answer on the inside. Use the riddles listed below or adapt your favorite elephant jokes.

Lift-ups are also an excellent way to add a little punch to fact review. Tape the riddles about the classroom, on lockers, on students desks or add one a day to the classroom door.

WHAT DO WE CALL FROGS WHO RIDE ON OCEAN LINERS?

(passengers)

WHAT IS THE BEST WAY TO KEEP FROGS FROM SMELLING?

(hold their noses)

WHY DOES A FROG LAY EGGS?

(Because if dropped they would break.)

IF YOU SEE TWENTY GREEN FROGS HOPPING DOWN THE STREET, WHAT TIME IS IT?

(nineteen after one)

HOW CAN YOU TELL IF FROGS HAVE BEEN IN YOUR REFRIGERATOR?

(by the hop marks in the butter)

lily pad leap

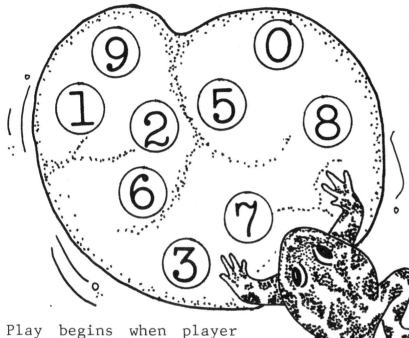

Lily Pad Leap is a math game designed to reinforce math facts. Begin by making a lily pad game board. Add circles all over the board with numbers on them as shown. Also prepare a stack of math fact cards. The answers to the math facts should be found in a circle on the playing board.

Play begins when player one turns over a math fact card and reads it out loud. The first player to find the answer on the board, covers it with one of his markers. Markers may be buttons, checkers, or small pieces of paper. The other player then turns over a card. The player with the most markers on the board at the end of the game wins. You will need to have different colored markers for each player.

Use a roll of tape to put hop marks on the floor of your classroom. Number them 1, 2, 3, 4 etc. Students must measure the distance from point 1 to point 2, etc. Each distance should be recorded.

Which student can frog hop the farthest? Just for fun finish your math with a frog-hopping contest.

PUPPET HOPPY

Frog puppets can be quickly made from small sized paper plates
and pieces of construction paper. Begin by having students paint
the plates green on both sides. Fold the dry plate in half as
shown. Add construction paper details. Use stand up paper for
the eyes. Even better would be to use cotton balls for the eyes.
They would really bulge. Students can add arms and legs and
a tongue as shown. The children can use the completed puppets
to answer teacher questions, recite poems they have learned
to the class, or have conversations with their friends.

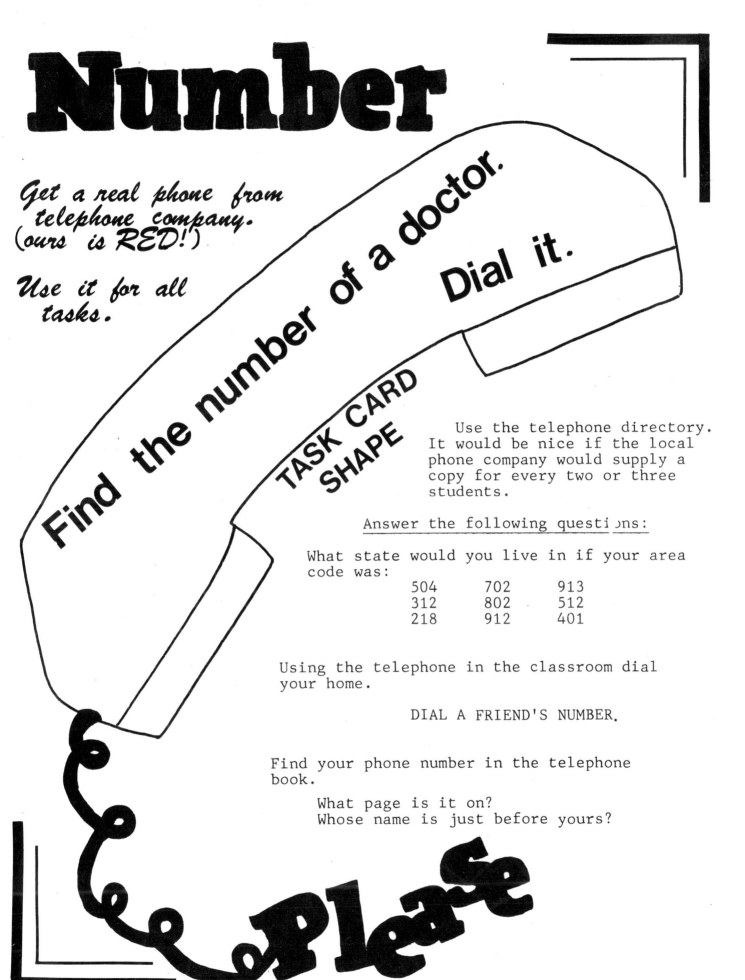

Number

Get a real phone from telephone company. (ours is RED!)

Use it for all tasks.

Find the number of a doctor. Dial it.

TASK CARD SHAPE

Use the telephone directory. It would be nice if the local phone company would supply a copy for every two or three students.

Answer the following questions:

What state would you live in if your area code was:

504	702	913
312	802	512
218	912	401

Using the telephone in the classroom dial your home.

DIAL A FRIEND'S NUMBER.

Find your phone number in the telephone book.

What page is it on?
Whose name is just before yours?

Please

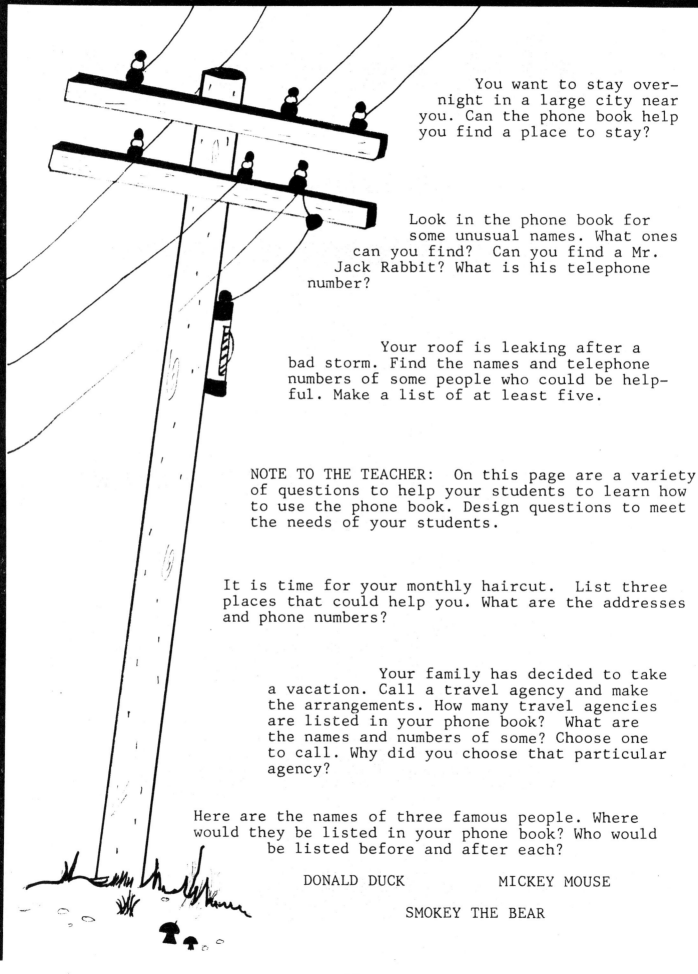

You want to stay over-
night in a large city near
you. Can the phone book help
you find a place to stay?

Look in the phone book for
some unusual names. What ones
can you find? Can you find a Mr.
Jack Rabbit? What is his telephone
number?

Your roof is leaking after a
bad storm. Find the names and telephone
numbers of some people who could be help-
ful. Make a list of at least five.

NOTE TO THE TEACHER: On this page are a variety
of questions to help your students to learn how
to use the phone book. Design questions to meet
the needs of your students.

It is time for your monthly haircut. List three
places that could help you. What are the addresses
and phone numbers?

Your family has decided to take
a vacation. Call a travel agency and make
the arrangements. How many travel agencies
are listed in your phone book? What are
the names and numbers of some? Choose one
to call. Why did you choose that particular
agency?

Here are the names of three famous people. Where
would they be listed in your phone book? Who would
be listed before and after each?

DONALD DUCK   MICKEY MOUSE

SMOKEY THE BEAR

TLL-ephone

For a real challenge give the students a number and see if they can think of a word that will equal that number.

Use the phone on this page or a real one to find the value of the words also listed at the bottom of this page. For example:

M – O – U – S – E

m = 6, o = 6, u = 8, s = 7, e = 3,

The word equals a total of 30.

dog _
orange _
recess _
tree _
apple _
rabbit _
number _
teacher _
operator _
pumpkin _
school _
light _
turtle _

OPERATOR

$\underline{4} + \underline{6} = \boxed{10}$ $\underline{} \; \underline{} = \bigcirc$ $\underline{} \; \underline{} = \bigcirc$

$\underline{} \; \underline{} = \bigcirc$ $\underline{} \; \underline{} = \bigcirc$ $\underline{} \; \underline{} = \bigcirc$

$\underline{} \; \underline{} = \bigcirc$ $\underline{} \; \underline{} = \bigcirc$ $\underline{} \; \underline{} = \bigcirc$

more...

$\underline{} + \underline{} + \underline{} = \bigcirc$ $\underline{} \; \underline{} \; \underline{} = \bigcirc$ $\underline{} + \underline{} + \underline{} = \bigcirc$

$\underline{} \; \underline{} = \bigcirc$ $\underline{} + \underline{} + \underline{} = \bigcirc$ $\underline{} \; \underline{} = \bigcirc$

$\underline{} \; \underline{} = \bigcirc$ $\underline{} \; \underline{} = \bigcirc$ $\underline{} + \underline{} + \underline{} = \bigcirc$

Some students may want to complete a worksheet similar to this one several times. Using the numbers on a telephone dial the students fill in the blanks and answers. Then operation signs are added. REMEMBER: Only the numbers on the telephone dial can be used.

STOP the PRESS!

Make each of the ideas presented on this page into a task card. Place the cards with a stack of newspapers that the students can use to answer the tasks.

Cut out a favorite action picture from the sports section and paste it on a piece of construction paper.

3

Find something that tells about winter.

(or spring or fall)

1

Cut out 1 picture.

Write words or a story about it.

2

Find letters of the alphabet. Cut them out and match them like this...

A a   Nn

Qq   Jj

4

Cut out a picture from the funnies section and write your own caption in a balloon you draw over the subject.

5

LOOK for five things that are on sale.

$5.75

6

Find out the best place to get the used car of your dreams. How much does it cost?

7

Find something about the weather.

11

Make a long list of words you can read.

8

Find out two times when you could watch the world news on TV.

9

Where can you get a new puppy?

10

STOP the PRESS!

Give child a newspaper.

It would be nice if each child could have a copy of the same newspaper.

Set a time limit of 10 to 20 minutes.

Let them skim the paper to find:

names of states	names of countries
names of stores	things to eat
names of famous people	things to wear
names of animals	4 syllable words
brand name products	

Use the next pages to write on.

OR

Mount on white paper.....then on a piece of newspaper as a background.

Use the sheets on the next page as samples. Make up a list of additional things to find in the newspaper. The above are only suggestions.

ALSO.....

For younger children we like to give a newspaper and circle all the words in a column or a part of a page and ask them to find certain things like: all the compound words or words with prefixes. This helps get the children to at least look at a newspaper and become familiar with it as a good reading experience.

CITIES

PEOPLE

STATES

WEST VIRGINIA

ANIMALS

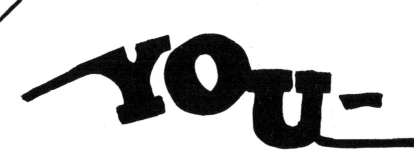

YOU-

This is a good center to have for your annual "open house." Some of the following activities can be placed on the child's desk. We suggest placing the silhoutte on the child's desk and let the parents try to find which desk belongs to their youngster. This is great fun and gives the parents something to do. After the parents look at the completed material it can be taken home. It is good public relations to give the parents something to take home on that special night. The sheet in this section entitled THIS IS WHERE I SIT is also placed on the child's desk.

Autographs:
Judi
June
Don
Gary
Toni

13"

Have each child collect autographs of his favorite people. Autographs from home, from school, from the neighborhood.

My name is _____.
I like ___ and ___.
I don't like _____.
I want to be _____.

11"

Using the light of an overhead projector we made the silhouette of each child. Tape a large sheet of black construction paper to a wall or the chalkboard. Have the child stand between the projector and the black paper. This is quick and easy and will delight parents. Mount the cutout silhouette on a piece of white paper.

← 12" →

The students can complete a simple information sheet. This can be taped to the mounted silhouette .

The Biggest
Number I Know
2,753

nique

Cut out this big "I" from white construction paper. Each student draws pictures of or writes the things that he/she can do. Tape to the child's desk.

←12"→

81

My Favorite Foods

Have children cut pictures from magazines or draw the things that they like to eat.

Superman

Popeye

Jaws

Steamroller

R2   D2

Worm

String
Bean

Jellyfish

Cut a seven foot flower as shown. Tie a long plastic tube (from your pharmacy) all the way up to the top. Tape a kitchen detergent bottle with the top dispenser broken off to the tube. Tape the top and tube together for a solid hold. The top of the tube must be open. The bottle of course is filled with water. The task card calls for the children to squeeze the bottle with the left hand then the right and then both hands to see how far they can push the water up the spout.

CORNER

List all sorts of fun levels for them to achieve. The flower is made from cardboard that is covered with contact paper or painted. Staple or tack to a bulletin board.

Have your students suggest names for the various levels of ability.

Mirror

Mirror

Be sure all necessary material for this project is easy to find.

WHAT TO DO

1. Look in the mirror.

2. Draw what you see with colors.

3. Fill in with the watercolors.

4. Cut out your face.

5. Glue it on a mirror.

6. Put EVERYTHING back in its place.

Precut the "face" paper and the mirrors.

NOTE TO THE TEACHER:

Print the above directions on a sheet of cardboard folded so that it stands.

Look in the mirror!
Look for something you have never seen before!

Look in the mirror....say AHHhhh! What do you see in the back of your throat? What is the thing that is pink and soft and moves? Can you make it move in funny ways?

Look at your teeth. How many do you have? Are any missing? Draw what you see on the tooth map. (One follows on the next page.)

Let your arms hang down. Where do your fingers touch? Make your arms do some different things. Move them about. What will they do?

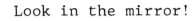

Stand straight. Make your knees move. Which ways can you move them?

Look at your eyes. Count your eyelashes. Can you count the hairs in your eyebrows or are they too thick? Could you count how many hairs are on your head? Why not? What do you see when you look at your eyes?

Make this task card shape.

Write a task on each one.

Find a full length mirror.

Let them perform in front of it.

YOU

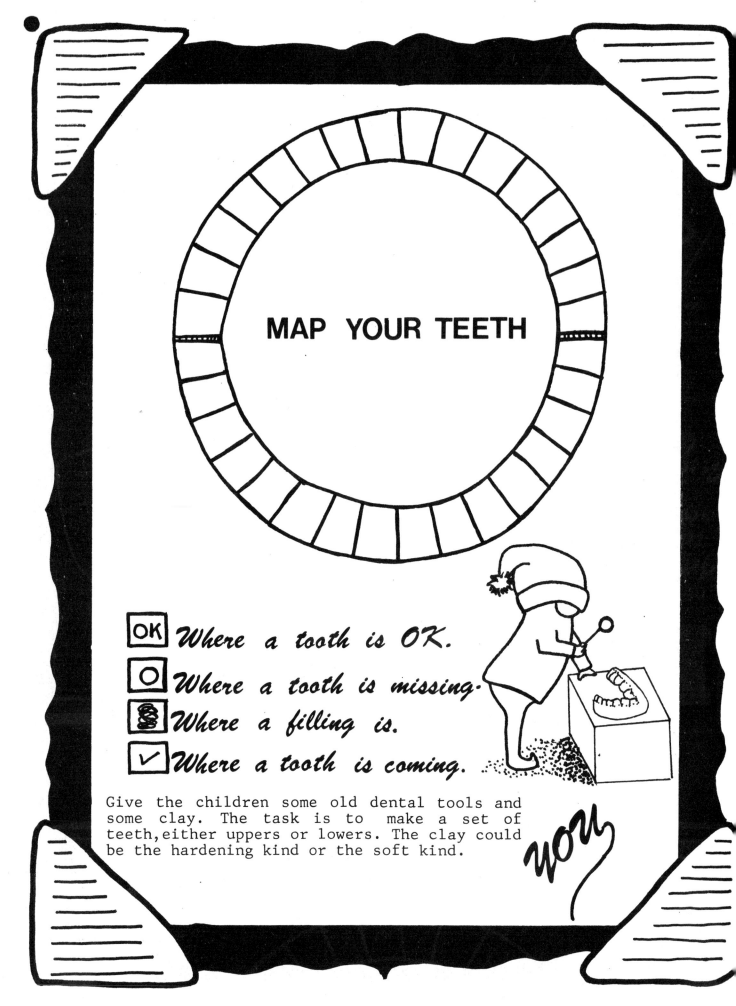

MAP YOUR TEETH

OK Where a tooth is OK.

O Where a tooth is missing.

Where a filling is.

✓ Where a tooth is coming.

Give the children some old dental tools and some clay. The task is to make a set of teeth, either uppers or lowers. The clay could be the hardening kind or the soft kind.

YOUR NOSE KNOWS

What do you like to smell? Look in magazines and cut out pictures of things you would like to smell. On a piece of paper draw a big nose. Paste some of the pictures you cut out around the nose. Now put the nose on your body cutout.

STUFF N' MOUTH

Stand in front of the mirror. Stick out your tongue, roll it around, let it hang out. Can you talk with it out? Keep your tongue still as you can. Can you talk that way? Look at your mouth. How is it shaped? Make different shapes with it. Draw your mouth on your body cutout.

WHAT'S IN A NAME

When you go home today, find out why you were given your name. Have fun with your name. Take your crayons and make your name in different colors. Paste the letters of your name on a strip of paper and then paste the strip across the tummy of your body cutout.

Make your name as colorful as you can.

NOTE TO THE TEACHER:

You might like to put out a variety of things for the children to taste while they are observing the mouth.

TEN FINGERS

Take a piece of paper and a crayon. Very carefully draw around both of your hands. Add the fingernails and other marks you see on your hands. Cut them out and paste them on your body cutout. On each of your fingers and thumbs list one thing that your hands can do.

HERE I AM

Take a large piece of paper and ask a friend to draw around YOU. Cut out the shape. Do not put anything on it. The next cards will tell you what to do.

1

JUST ME

READ THE POEM.

Now color in the skin on your cutout.

2

THE EYES HAVE IT

Take the eye chart. Go to the mirror and look at your eyes. Watch your eyes. Cover the rest of your face with a piece of paper... everything but your eyes. Smile. Did your eyes change? Make other expressions. Watch your eyes. Draw your eyes on your body cutout.

3

A"HAIRY" TIME

Look in the mirror. Look at your hair. What color is it? Is it wavy, straight, or curly? Draw your hair on the body cutout.

Find the page with the charts and a "measuring" body.

4

Make the charts on this page from white tagboard
or white railroad board. Score them as shown.

The students will take a mirror
and identify the color of
their hair and then put their
name in the proper column. The
same will be done for the type
of hair chart.

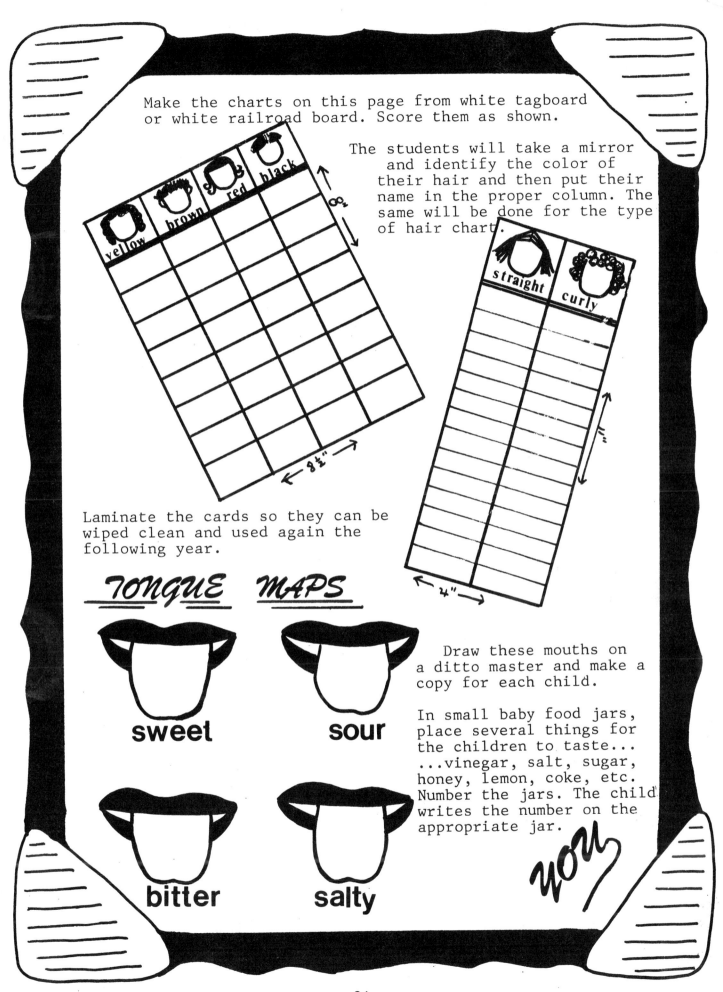

yellow | brown | red | black

8"

8½"

straight | curly

1"

4"

Laminate the cards so they can be
wiped clean and used again the
following year.

TONGUE MAPS

sweet

sour

bitter

salty

Draw these mouths on
a ditto master and make a
copy for each child.

In small baby food jars,
place several things for
the children to taste...
...vinegar, salt, sugar,
honey, lemon, coke, etc.
Number the jars. The child
writes the number on the
appropriate jar.

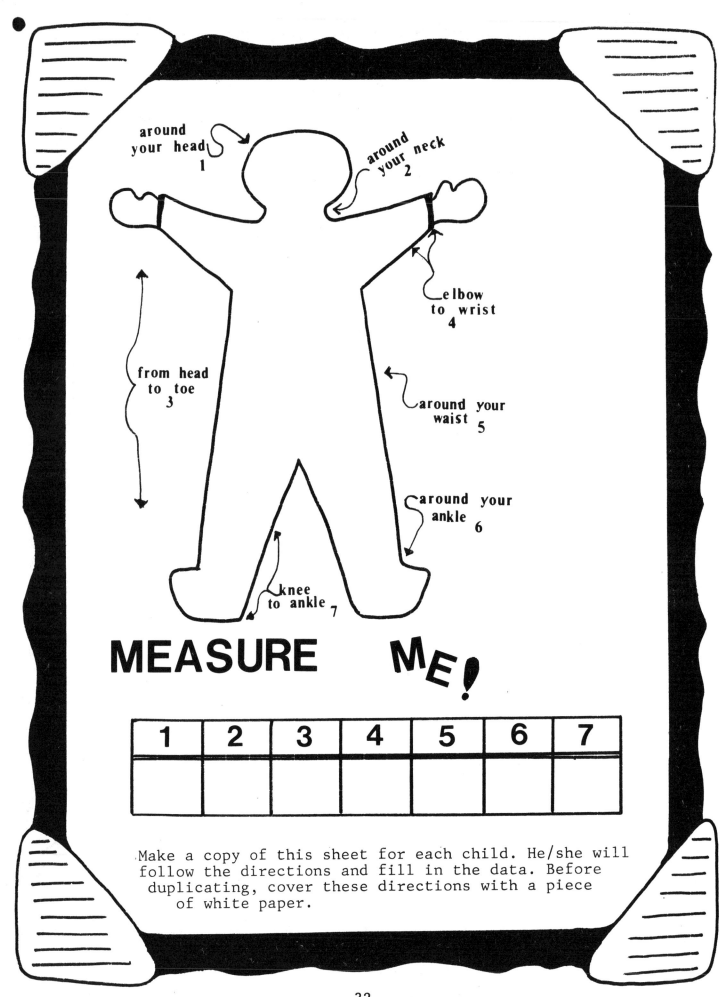

around
your head
1

around
your neck
2

elbow
to wrist
4

from head
to toe
3

around your
waist
5

around your
ankle
6

knee
to ankle 7

MEASURE ME!

1	2	3	4	5	6	7

Make a copy of this sheet for each child. He/she will
follow the directions and fill in the data. Before
duplicating, cover these directions with a piece
of white paper.

YOU-nique

Name

Age

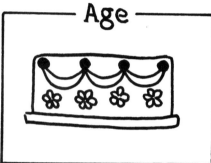

Fingerprint

Favorite Color

 Height

Hair color

 Weight

Number of Teeth

Eye Color

How do you feel today?

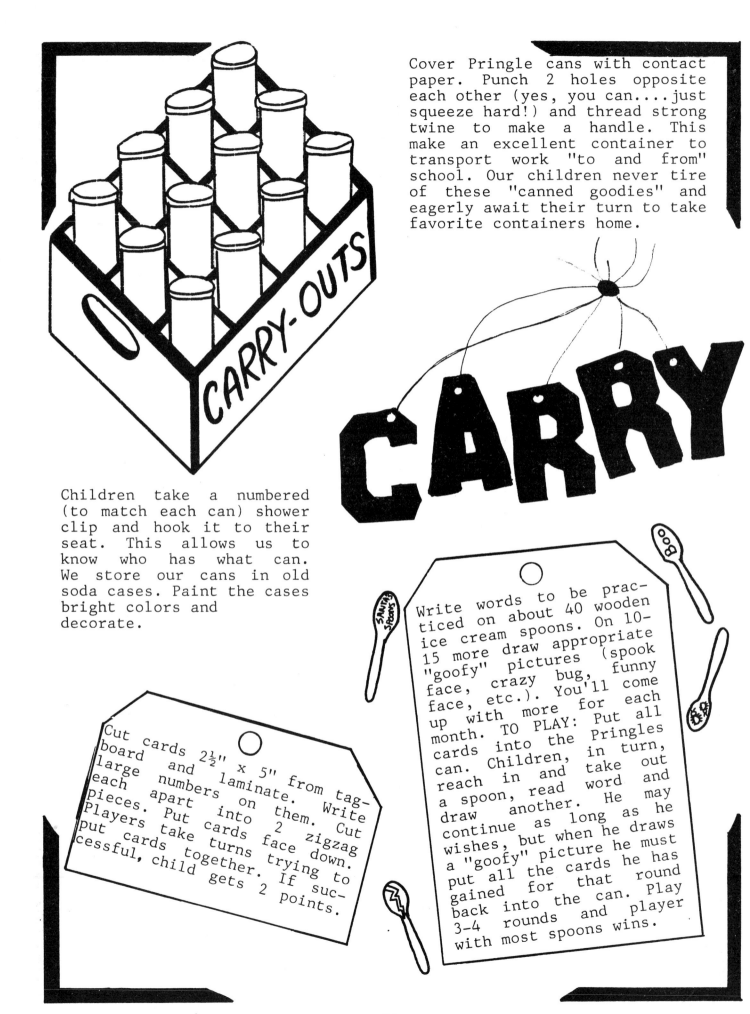

CARRY-OUTS

Cover Pringle cans with contact paper. Punch 2 holes opposite each other (yes, you can....just squeeze hard!) and thread strong twine to make a handle. This make an excellent container to transport work "to and from" school. Our children never tire of these "canned goodies" and eagerly await their turn to take favorite containers home.

CARRY

Children take a numbered (to match each can) shower clip and hook it to their seat. This allows us to know who has what can. We store our cans in old soda cases. Paint the cases bright colors and decorate.

Cut cards 2½" x 5" from tagboard and laminate. Write large numbers on them. Cut each apart into 2 zigzag pieces. Put cards face down. Players take turns trying to put cards together. If successful, child gets 2 points.

Write words to be practiced on about 40 wooden ice cream spoons. On 10-15 more draw appropriate "goofy" pictures (spook face, crazy bug, funny face, etc.). You'll come up with more for each month. TO PLAY: Put all cards into the Pringles can. Children, in turn, reach in and take out a spoon, read word and draw another. He may continue as long as he wishes, but when he draws a "goofy" picture he must put all the cards he has gained for that round back into the can. Play 3-4 rounds and player with most spoons wins.

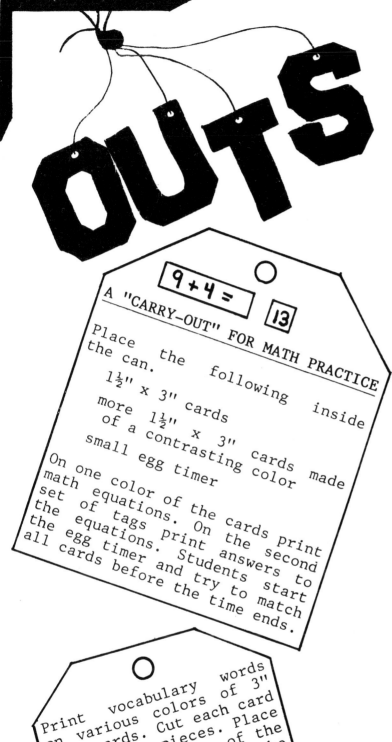

OUTS

A "CARRY-OUT" FOR MATH PRACTICE

$9 + 4 =$ ⬜ 13

Place the following inside the can.

1½" x 3" cards

more 1½" x 3" cards made of a contrasting color

small egg timer

On one color of the cards print math equations. On the second set of tags print answers to the equations. Students start the egg timer and try to match all cards before the time ends.

Print vocabulary words on various colors of 3" x 5" cards. Cut each card into puzzle pieces. Place all puzzle pieces of the various colors into the "carry-out". The task is to make the puzzles and then pronounce the vocabulary word. Parents can check the pronunciation of the words and ask the child to use the word in a sentence.

Type all directions on circles made of manila folder. The circles should be a size to fit inside the Pringles Can. The circles can be laminated and placed inside the lid of the can. A dab of glue will help hold it in place.

When the cans arrive at home with the children the parents will know immediately what task is to be completed.

Tic Tac Toe

Laminate a 6" x 6" piece of paper on which you have drawn a Tic-Tac-Toe grid. In each section of the grid print a vocabulary word. Make six 2" squares each with a large "X" on it. Make six 2" squares each with a large "O" on it. Place all this material in a "carry-out" can. Players take turns pronouncing the words and placing the "X's" and "O's. The winner is the first to Tic-Tac-Toe. Several grids can be placed in the same can.

HERE IS HOW YOUR

CANS WILL LOOK!

 MATCH-UP

Make a can filled with about 25-30 of these designs:

strawberries – tops   dogs – bones
rabbits – their tails   mice – cheese
butterfly – center of body

Make each of these out of colored tagboard. Laminate after putting facts or words on. Children match math set with answer, 9+7 = 16 or match the word with its definition, or match which words rhyme, which are antonyms, states and capitals or capital and lower case letters.

BINGO!!

Make a bingo card on a piece of 7½" x 9" piece of railroad board. In the bingo squares write the following phonic sounds. Place a sound in various positions on the various bingo cards. Don't forget FREE!

ie   oe   oy   wa   ee   ue   ay
ing ome ete oi   oa   oa   at
in   ipe ea   ile er   ir   ur
ole ite ime ike ale ai   on

Put each sound on a card for the caller. Place beans in the Pringle can to use as markers. Play just like bingo.

For this game spelling is not the focus. Hearing the sound is what counts.

You'll think of more!

SCRAMBLE

On 1½" squares of tagboard print the letters of the alphabet, five of each consonant and 8 or 10 of each vowel. Place in can and shake them up. First child takes out 2 cards for the first round only. Second child does the same, and so on until each player has two cards. For the next 4 or 5 rounds each player draws only one card. Everytime a word can be made the player lays it down. After 4 or 5 rounds the player with the most words wins. The game can be played several times.

Duplicate some of the sheets and games you find in activity books from the various publishers. These worksheets can be rolled in placed in the various Pringle cans.

Short stories to read can be put in some of the cans as well as some of the dittoed sheets you design and duplicate.

APPLE HAPPY

If you are looking for FRUIT-ful learning activities and BUSHELS of learning fun you might try a study of apples. In the early fall apples, small, tall, round, red, green and yellow are available at roadside stands and super-markets across the nation. Use apples to reinforce reading and language arts skills. Use apples to help children apply math skills. Use apples to spark creative thinking through apple art and writing projects. And....most of all eat and enjoy a few. Remember one a day will keep the doldrums away.

Treat your students to a cup of cold apple cider just after recess when they are hot and tired and need to refresh and relax. At this time show the filmstrip, How Apples Grow. It is available from The International Apple Institute, 2430 Pennsylvania Avenue, NW, Washington D.C., 20037 for just $3.00. Prepare a filmstrip guide sheet (using a fill-in-the-blank approach) with the filmstrip. All informa-tion on the guide sheet should pertain to the filmstrip. Allow time for the stu-dents to read through the guide sheet at least once before the viewing takes place. You can clarify major concepts and provide help with tricky vocabulary words. The guide sheet will help focus attention on the filmstrip and success for everyone is almost assured.

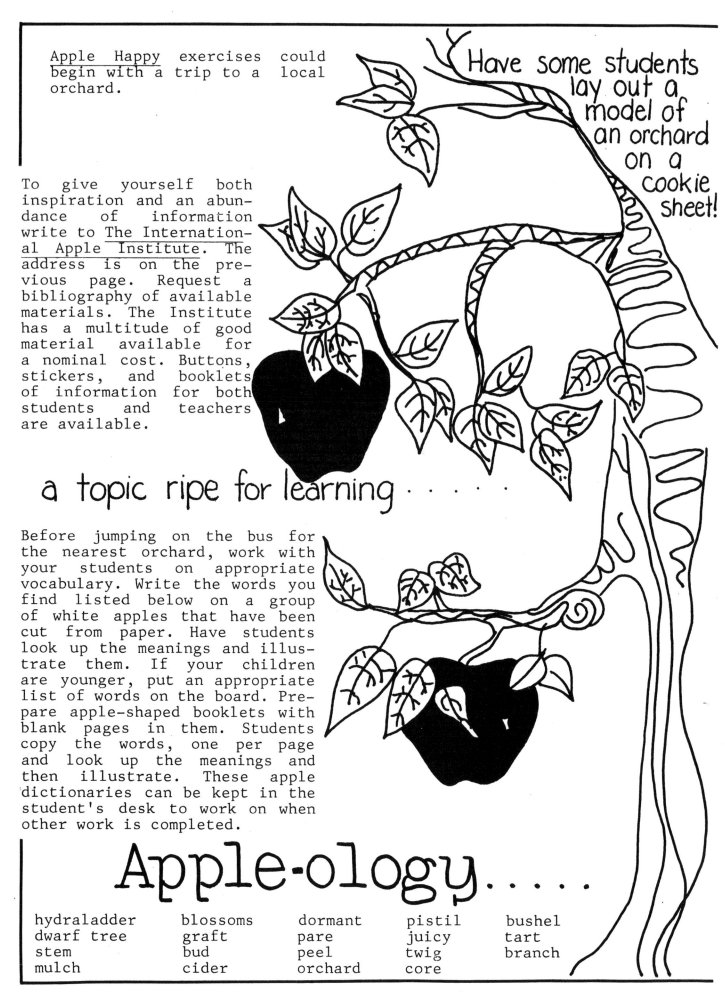

Apple Happy exercises could begin with a trip to a local orchard.

Have some students lay out a model of an orchard on a cookie sheet!

To give yourself both inspiration and an abundance of information write to The International Apple Institute. The address is on the previous page. Request a bibliography of available materials. The Institute has a multitude of good material available for a nominal cost. Buttons, stickers, and booklets of information for both students and teachers are available.

a topic ripe for learning . . . . .

Before jumping on the bus for the nearest orchard, work with your students on appropriate vocabulary. Write the words you find listed below on a group of white apples that have been cut from paper. Have students look up the meanings and illustrate them. If your children are younger, put an appropriate list of words on the board. Prepare apple-shaped booklets with blank pages in them. Students copy the words, one per page and look up the meanings and then illustrate. These apple dictionaries can be kept in the student's desk to work on when other work is completed.

Apple-ology.....

hydraladder	blossoms	dormant	pistil	bushel
dwarf tree	graft	pare	juicy	tart
stem	bud	peel	twig	branch
mulch	cider	orchard	core	

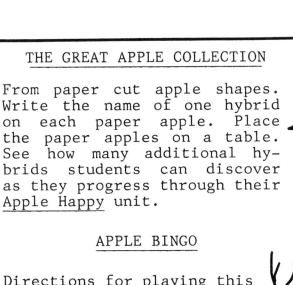

THE GREAT APPLE COLLECTION

From paper cut apple shapes. Write the name of one hybrid on each paper apple. Place the paper apples on a table. See how many additional hybrids students can discover as they progress through their Apple Happy unit.

APPLE BINGO

Directions for playing this game can be found on the following two pages. It is a walking bingo game that can be played as students are on their field trip to the orchard.

FROM ORCHARD TO STORE

When you return from the orchard use a roll of shelf paper and have students illustrate the sequence of events that an apple proceeds through from blossom to grocery store.

FOUR SEASONS OF THE APPLE TREE

Cut out a large circle from a sheet of butcher paper. Divide the circle into four pie shaped sections. Have the students illustrate how an apple tree looks in each of the four seasons. Trim the completed circle to a tree shape and attach to a tree trunk made of brown craft or construction paper.

in the orchard

A trip to a nearby apple orchard is the perfect autumn outing. Recruit three or four parents to help. Each parent can be responsible for five or six students. Make temporary clipboards from cardboard and staple the walking bingo sheets to the clipboards. Tuck an extra pencil or crayon in your pocket just in case someone forgets.

Walking BINGO

a green apple	bee hives	a tree with yellow apples	a tree with storm damage	a cider press
a dwarf tree	windfall apples	hydra-ladder	a man picking apples	white coating of spray on apples
apples ready for sale	washed apples	free free	a full bushel of apples	an apple leaf
a man driving a load of apples	apples being washed	hay at tree base used for mulch	large red apples	protection around base of the tree
a tractor	small red apples	a worm	apples being stored	crate of apples

for older students

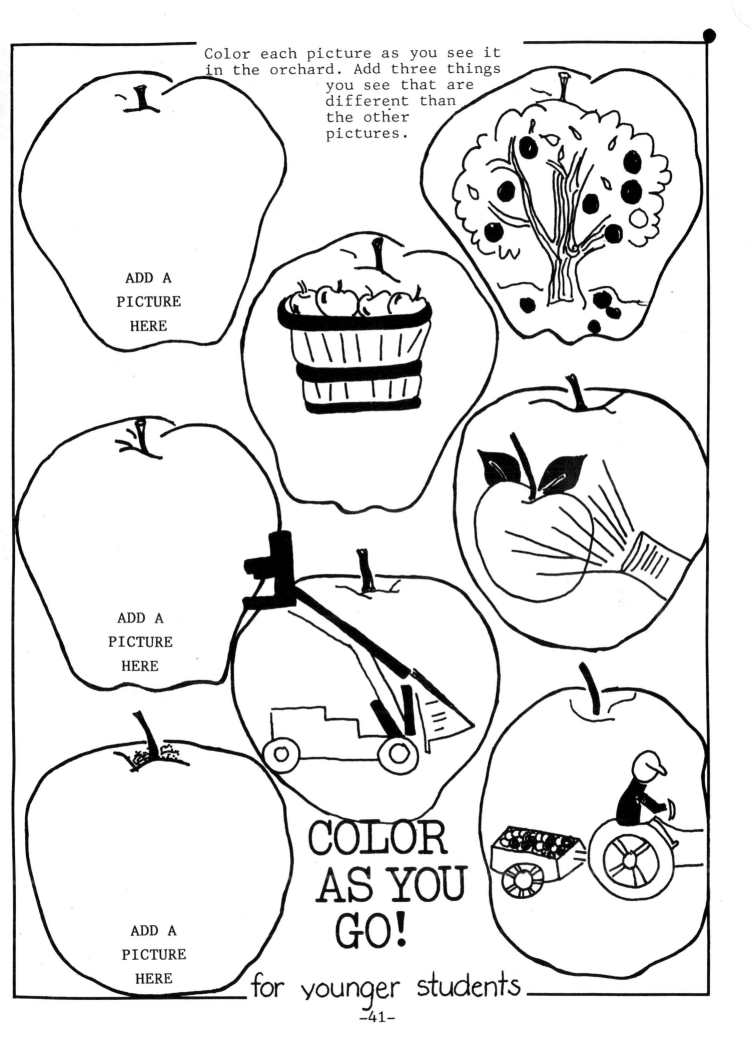

Color each picture as you see it in the orchard. Add three things you see that are different than the other pictures.

ADD A PICTURE HERE

ADD A PICTURE HERE

ADD A PICTURE HERE

COLOR AS YOU GO!

for younger students

APPLE HAPPY ART

Develop the Van Gogh in each child by setting up an apple still life. Share famous still life pictures with the students when they have completed their work. Don't forget Cézanne's The Big Apples.

Apple-y Prints

Begin by spreading finger paint in a cookie sheet. Have each student in turn draw an apple tree or other apple related picture. The child can use only one finger to paint. Lay a sheet of construction paper over the top of the completed finger painting. Smooth down with the flat part of the hand. Peel the paper off and let it dry. Students color in the white spaces using pastels.

Watch student creativity BLOSSOM!

3-D Trees

Use 6" x 9" pieces of green construction paper and have students cut two tree shapes at one time. Add apples where desired. Slit as shown. Stand these trees on bookshelves and tables about the classroom. If you have access to large sheets of tri-wall cardboard, make a room-sized tree by preparing a pattern from brown butcher paper and cutting the shape with a saber saw. Slit and stand in the corner of your room.

Make the project extra interesting by providing colored chalk for the kids to use.

Apple Windows

Sandwich a piece of colored tissue or cellophane between two apple-shaped frames for light-catchers. Hang about the room and in the windows and much color will be provided.

Apple Batik

Combine manila construction paper with bright crayons or oil pastels and wash with tempera paint to make apple batiks. Have the students draw large and small apples with bright green, yellow and red crayons or pastels all over the paper. Then have the students crunch the papers and smooth them out on their desks. Next, using a wide paint brush and a thin tempera wash of green or black, the students paint the crayon picture. When dry, mount on apple colored paper. Crunch lines will be darker.

MORE

Apple mobile

Applemobiles are quickly made from three 14 inch strips of yellow, red or green construction paper. Have students lay them in a star shape as shown and attach with brass fasteners. Form the apple by joining the top edges with a brass fastener. Add construction paper leaves and a stem. Hang or pile in an apple basket.

bottom

Stuff & Fluff

Cut tissue paper into apple shapes to form this apple pillow. Use scraps of tissue paper to stuff. Hang completed apples in the hall outside your classroom door. But, watch out for wandering William Tells!

Apple Patches

If you have scraps of tissue paper in apple colors this project will be a nice way to use them. Begin by having students draw the outline of an apple on a 4" x 6" piece of paper. Students then lay pieces of waxed paper on top of the outline. Next dip small pieces of tissue in polymer medium (gloss) and lay on the waxed paper. The apple outline should serve as a guide. When the first layer is dry a second layer should be cut and glued. After adding a third layer of tissue use a marker to outline the apple. Add a construction paper leaf and stem.

...Apple Happy Art

Plate Portholes

In a "paper plate porthole" students can draw their favorite apple treat or something they enjoyed during the field trip to the orchard. Begin by having each student paint two paper plates a delicious red color. Cut out the center of one plate as shown. The student's drawing can then be placed inside. Staple the edges together, add green leaves and hang with a piece of green yarn.

Core Mobiles

Have some students make apple core mobiles to hang among the plate portholes. Cut two tops, two centers and two bottom pieces. Use red, green or yellow paper for the top and bottom pieces and white for the center. Add seeds with black crayon, marker or cut and glue small bits of black construction paper.

Easy Over & Under

Apple place mats can be made by having students cut a large piece of construction paper into an apple shape. Add vertical slits. Students can weave in strips of a contrasting color. This is a project that each child can keep in his desk and can work on to productively fill those moments when other work is completed.

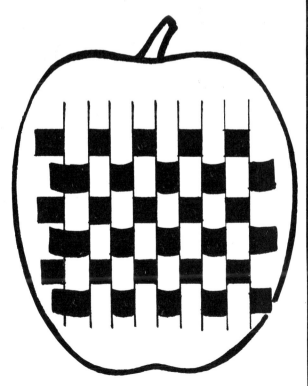

Apple Happy Tasks

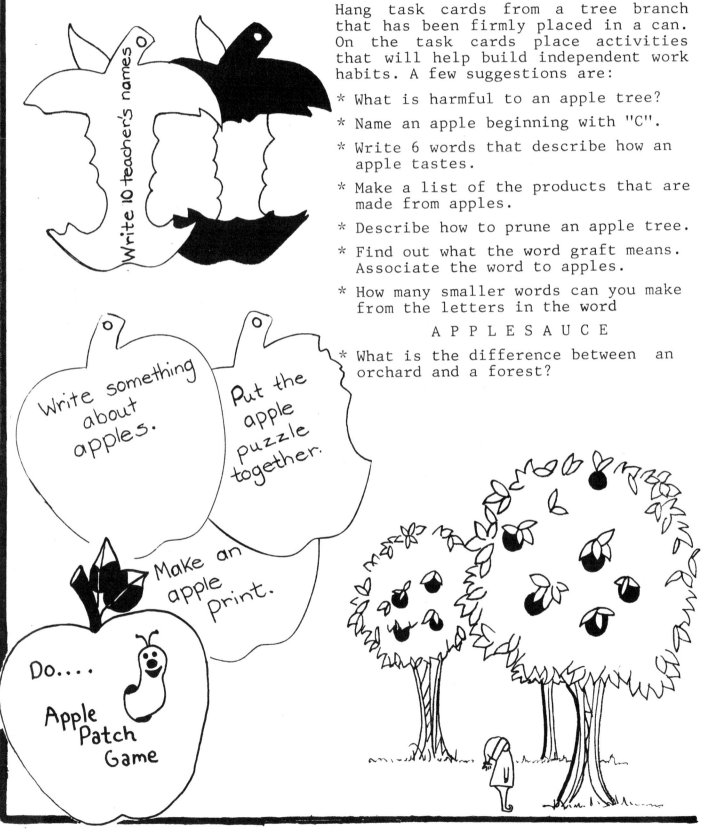

Write 10 teacher's names

Write something about apples.

Put the apple puzzle together.

Make an apple print.

Do.... Apple Patch Game

Hang task cards from a tree branch that has been firmly placed in a can. On the task cards place activities that will help build independent work habits. A few suggestions are:

* What is harmful to an apple tree?

* Name an apple beginning with "C".

* Write 6 words that describe how an apple tastes.

* Make a list of the products that are made from apples.

* Describe how to prune an apple tree.

* Find out what the word graft means. Associate the word to apples.

* How many smaller words can you make from the letters in the word

       A P P L E S A U C E

* What is the difference between an orchard and a forest?

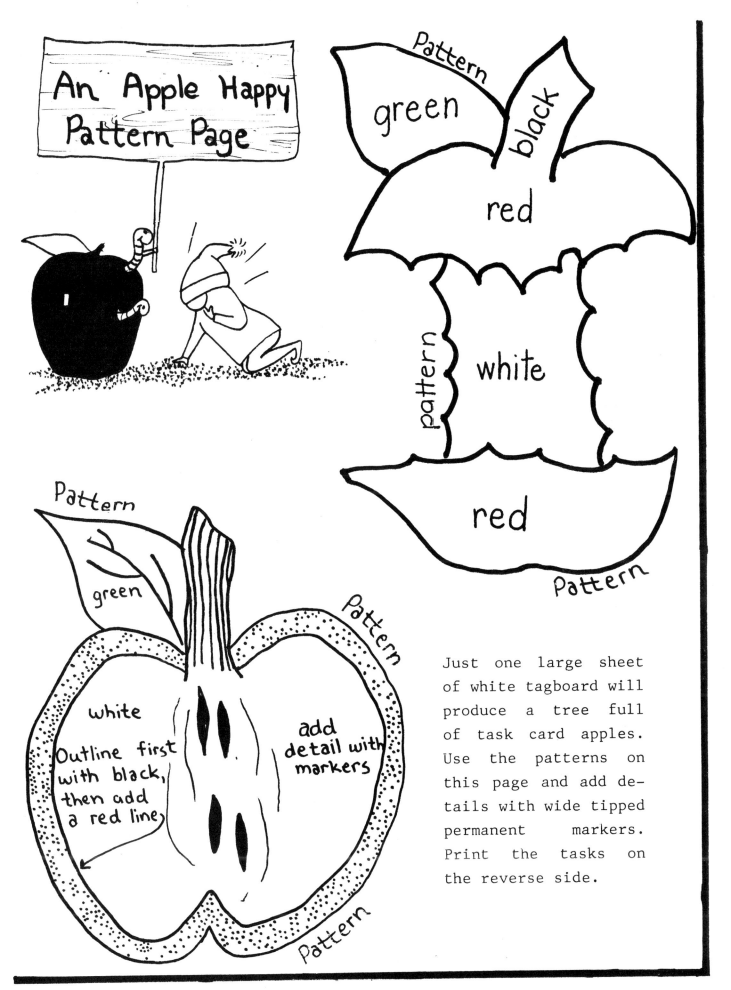

An Apple Happy Pattern Page

Pattern green black
red

Pattern white

Pattern red

Pattern green white

Outline first with black, then add a red line

add detail with markers

Pattern

Pattern

Just one large sheet of white tagboard will produce a tree full of task card apples. Use the patterns on this page and add details with wide tipped permanent markers. Print the tasks on the reverse side.

Apple Happy Reading

Divide the class into groups. Have the groups compose as many
A.– P.– P.– L.– E.
sentences as they can

A P <u>retty</u>

P eacock L <u>aid</u>

E <u>ggs</u>

WATCH YOUR STUDENTS "BRANCH OUT" INTO NEW LEARNING WITH:

<u>Where the Wild Apples Grow</u>,
John Hawkinson, Albert
Whitman Co., Chicago, 1967

<u>Apples</u>, Hogrogian, Nonny, MacMillian, New York,

<u>Apples: How They Grow</u>, McMillan, Houghton Mifflin,
Boston, 1979.

<u>The Apple War</u>, Bernice Meyers, Parents Press, New York.

<u>A Moment In Time</u>, Rothman, Scroll Press, New York, 1972.

<u>Rain Makes Applesauce</u>, Scheer, Holiday House, New York.

<u>The Apple and Other Fruits</u>, Selsam, Wm. Morrow & Co

Read <u>Appleseed Farm</u>,
Nashville, Abington Press,
1958

Fill a bushel basket full of books appropriate for your student's reading ability. When a student reads a book he can write the title of the book and his name on a paper apple and hang it on a bulletin board tree. When the class has accumulated 75 apples it's a kick-ball game or special recess surprise.

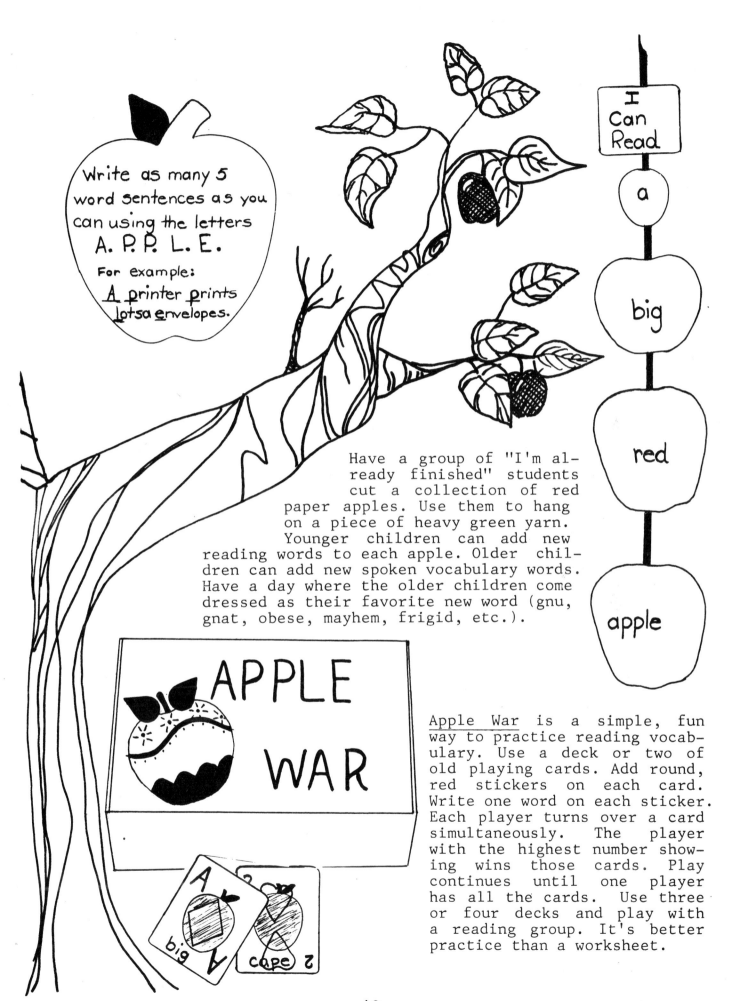

Write as many 5 word sentences as you can using the letters A. P. P. L. E.

For example:
A printer prints lotsa envelopes.

I Can Read

a

big

red

apple

Have a group of "I'm already finished" students cut a collection of red paper apples. Use them to hang on a piece of heavy green yarn. Younger children can add new reading words to each apple. Older children can add new spoken vocabulary words. Have a day where the older children come dressed as their favorite new word (gnu, gnat, obese, mayhem, frigid, etc.).

APPLE WAR

Apple War is a simple, fun way to practice reading vocabulary. Use a deck or two of old playing cards. Add round, red stickers on each card. Write one word on each sticker. Each player turns over a card simultaneously. The player with the highest number showing wins those cards. Play continues until one player has all the cards. Use three or four decks and play with a reading group. It's better practice than a worksheet.

Adapt some of the games on these two pages to work your students are doing in their language arts classes. Change the skills to meet the needs of your students.

READ: <u>The Apple and Other Fruits,</u> Wm. Morrow, New York, 1973.

LANGUAGE ARTS

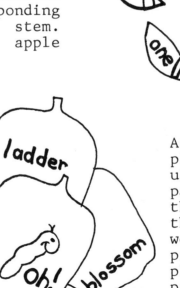

Apple Patch is a simple matching activity. Put the one item to be matched on the front part of the apple and its corresponding element on the leaf or stem. Store in a box or burlap apple bag.

As the Worm Turns is played to review vocabulary. Cut a stack of paper apples, at least thirty-six. On about thirty write vocabulary words. On six draw a picture of a worm. To play, stack-up all the paper apples with the word and worm-side down. The first student reads the apples until he comes to a worm. The student gets one point for each word read correctly. The student must stop reading when he turns over a worm card. The reader with the most points wins. Have students try keeping a running score and play against themselves, each time trying to do better. Store game in a paper bag to which you've added an apple decoration.

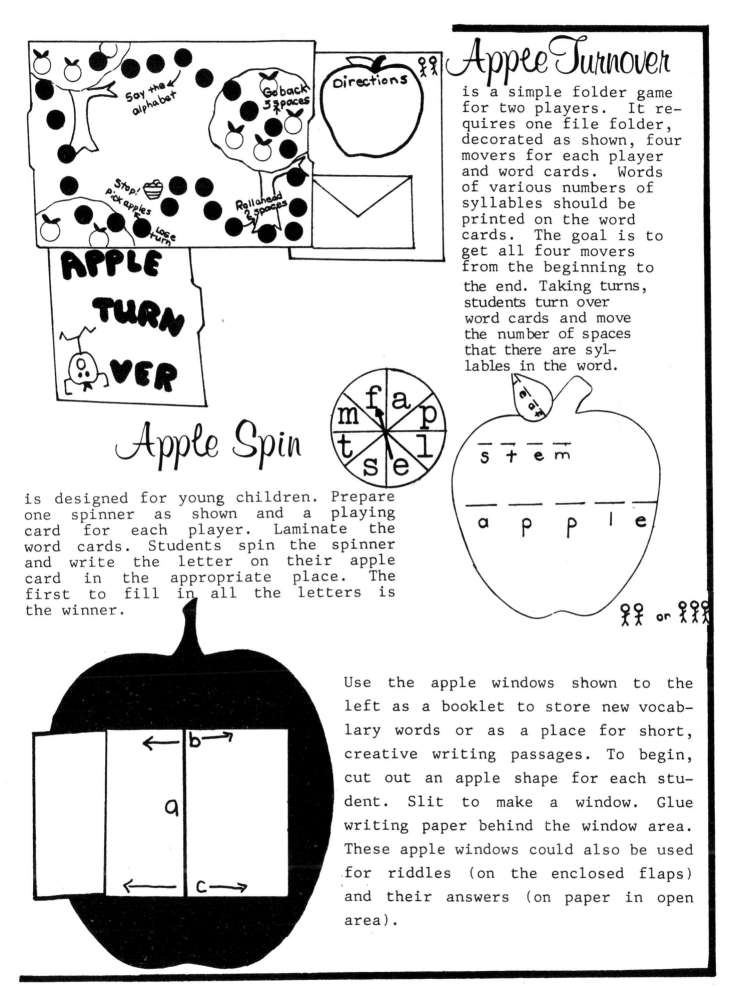

Apple Turnover

is a simple folder game for two players. It requires one file folder, decorated as shown, four movers for each player and word cards. Words of various numbers of syllables should be printed on the word cards. The goal is to get all four movers from the beginning to the end. Taking turns, students turn over word cards and move the number of spaces that there are syllables in the word.

Apple Spin

is designed for young children. Prepare one spinner as shown and a playing card for each player. Laminate the word cards. Students spin the spinner and write the letter on their apple card in the appropriate place. The first to fill in all the letters is the winner.

Use the apple windows shown to the left as a booklet to store new vocabulary words or as a place for short, creative writing passages. To begin, cut out an apple shape for each student. Slit to make a window. Glue writing paper behind the window area. These apple windows could also be used for riddles (on the enclosed flaps) and their answers (on paper in open area).

AppleHappy

language arts

Place a book and a recording of the story of Johnny Appleseed in a red pocket folder for the students to read and listen to on their own. In the empty folder place a follow-up worksheet. For younger children place a picture for them to color.

JOHNNY APPLESEED

Match-its!

red blue gray

one	six	nine	eleven
four	two	thirteen	zero
fifteen	five	seven	three
twelve	eight	fourteen	ten

B	P	D	E
N	M	Q	F
C	O	H	G
T	J	L	V

f   9
b   j   t   11   6   4

Make a collection of apple match-ups similar to those shown. If the students are older, present states and the capitals, homonyms and advanced math problems. Store in manila envelopes.

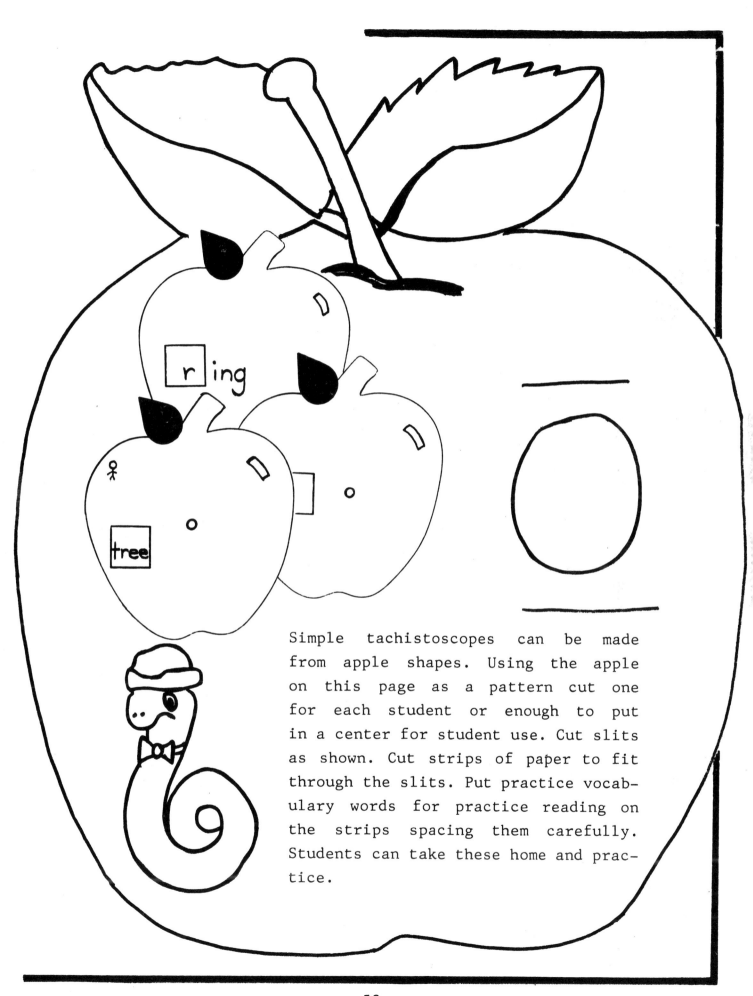

Simple tachistoscopes can be made from apple shapes. Using the apple on this page as a pattern cut one for each student or enough to put in a center for student use. Cut slits as shown. Cut strips of paper to fit through the slits. Put practice vocabulary words for practice reading on the strips spacing them carefully. Students can take these home and practice.

Use standard size construction paper to make learning place mats for young children. The place mats are actually giant task cards. They also structure the space on which students will work. Put one place mat at each place at a table. Materials needed to complete the task can be placed in a small container at the top of the place mat. Students follow the simple written directions, use the materials, and know where to return the materials. In Addition, "place mat learning" limits the number of students working on one project.

Make an apple movie.

Make an apple cookie.

Print the ABC's.

Put a border on the construction paper sheets with brightly colored markers. Write directions at the bottom of each mat as shown. You might provide apple-shaped writing paper for writing activities. Cookie cutters, rolling pins and play dough to make cookies will develop small muscle coordination. Stamp pads and letter stamps are all that is needed to stamp out new words. Be sure to laminate each place mat. The place mats are easy to store and get ready and provide hours of learning time.

A bushel, a peck or a bag of apples can contain many fruitful math learning activities.

Give each student an apple and the task of making an apple poster.

Stand a bushel basket (empty or full) on a table covered with a checkered table cloth and motivate creative thinking. Lead a discussion about capacity. How many apples would fit? How much would they weigh? Would a bushel of applesauce weigh more than a bushel of apples?

Motivate the students toward logical thinking activities as described on the next few pages.

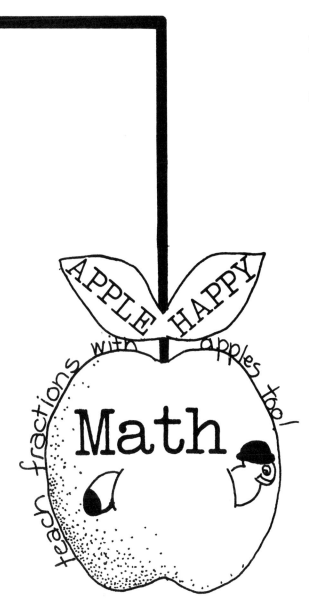

Apple Pie Order

Begin with a stack of pizza boards or construction paper circles. Add "apple pie" details. You are now ready for a stepping-stone sequence activity. Write numerals (appropriate for your students' level) on each "pie." Use single-digit numbers for first graders and six-digit numbers for fourth graders. Make a path from one point in the classroom to another. Students place circles in order along the path.

Logically... Apples

The Poison Apple, Apple Side by Sider, and Apples 23 are three simple thinking games. Try them instead of drill exercises at the end of each math period for a week or two. All you need is one copy for each pair of children and buttons or beans for markers.

Spray an old bread box shiny red and add the letters as shown. Now you have a perfect storage place for measuring, logic games, and necessary equipment. Check rummage sales, flea markets or your local second hand store for an old bread box.

to make....

Use one of the apples on this page for a pattern. Cut twelve bright red apples.

Also cut one green, poison apple. Use colored paper or contact paper to add the stem and leaf details.

Laminate all thirteen pieces and store in a small basket.

Poison Apple

to play...

Two students lay out the thirteen apples on a table, desk or the floor.

Each player takes turns taking either one or two apples avoiding THE POISON APPLE.

The player forced to take the poison apple loses the game.

a Sleeping Beauty favorite!

Apples 23!

DIRECTIONS: Each player will need 8 markers. Buttons or even squares of paper will work well. The object of the game is to be the player to get to the sum of 23. Player one places one of his markers on a number and says the number out loud. The second player places one of his markers on another number, mentally adding it to the previous total. He says that sum out loud. Play continues until one player reaches EXACTLY 23. For older children change the numerals from 1-4 to 5-8. For variety, have students <u>begin</u> with 23 and subtract to zero.

Apple Side-by-Sider

To play this game, provide one copy of the board for each pair of children. Each child will also need his own color of buttons or other markers. The object is for one player to place four of his markers in a row vertically, horizontally or diagonally. Students take turns placing one marker on any apple on the board. The first player to put four markers in a row, wins. Try three markers in a row for younger children.

see following page

Apple Posters

Provide a real apple for each student. Use as many varieties as you can. Also give each student a large sheet of white construction paper to use as an apple poster. Have students draw a picture of their apple in the center of the poster. Then using a string or tape measure, have students add the following information to their poster:

    the circumference
    the weight
    four things heavier
    four things lighter
    number of bites to the core
    number of seeds in the core
    length in millimeters of stem

Hang all posters about the classroom and have students graph the various bits of information.

Put a bushel, dish, or bucket of apples in a place where all students can see. Have students estimate the number of apples. Count to see who was closest by grouping in ones, tens, and hundreds. Take an empty bushel basket to the gym and find out how many balls fit in it. How many books fit? Let students make a list of all the different ways to fill a bushel. What can it hold?

A Bushel and a Peck

Apple Side-by-Sider

(directions on preceding page)

Apple time is the BEST time to cook with children. Applesauce is a standby. Try at least one of these interesting and nutritious treats. Maybe a parent or your principal will help.

APPLE HAPPY

Cooking
delicious learning!

Cut apples in boat-shaped wedges as shown. Slip a toothpick and hold a piece of cheese to each wedge.

Caramel apples are a traditional treat, but can be costly. Try spreading peanut butter on apple slices and making circle apple sandwiches. An inexpensive, healthy treat for kids.

APPLE FUN-DO is a simple recipe for children. Melt about ½ pound of Swiss cheese with 1 can of cheddar cheese soup. Have children dip apple chunks in the FUN-DO.

Let children do a little pie-baking with apples they have picked themselves. Use frozen pie crusts from your favorite supermarket. Mix the apple slices with sugar and cinnamon. Fill the crust and bake until done. The smell makes the effort worth it!

Taffy Apple Happy

how to.....

A collection of paper caramel apples can be a motivating learning aid. Use the drawing on this page as a pattern. The caramel top shown can be cut separately. Cut 36 tops from brown paper. Trace around the apple section and cut 36 apples. Write half of the match on the caramel section and the other half on the apple. Laminate two tops together and two bottoms together. DO NOT LAMINATE SINGLY, you want to create pockets. Slit a small opening in the bottom of the apple section and insert a stick. A dab of glue will make it secure. In the caramel section, slit the entire lower edge so it will slip over the top of the apple section.

pattern

what to.....

synonyms

antonyms

homonyms

upper/lower case letters

sight words/pictures

phonics skills

sentences/missing letters

cause/effect statements

abbreviations and source

book titles/authors

flags/countries

math facts/answers

color words/colors

compound words

states/capitals

...slip a birthday apple in each student's desk or locker

...find a friend or fellow teacher to dress as Johnny Appleseed and drop by your classroom

...bake an apple birthday cake

...make apple shaped birthday cards for Johnny

...write and perform a play about the life of Johnny

...drink apple cider at the birthday party

...everyone can wear an apple shaped nametag

APPLE HAPPY

Johnny Appleseed
a core of ideas to use with other folk heroes!

Celebrate his September 26th birthday by:

Students working independently can read at least two versions and list similarities and differences in the plots and characterizations.

Younger children can listen to two recorded versions and as a group make a list of likenesses and differences on the chalkboard.

Inexpensive recordings and books can be found in most discount stores.

Walt Disney Records has a version that is quite different from many.

Compare Versions

The stories of folk heroes vary, sometimes greatly, from version to version. Help students track down as many versions of the story of Johnny Appleseed as can be found in your school and libraries.

Before the students have been exposed to pictures of Johnny Appleseed have them form mental pictures of what he looks like, then display several publishers' illustrations of Johnny. Does he always look the same? Why? Why not?

The real name of <u>JOHNNY APPLESEED</u> is John Chapman. He lived in the 1800's, roaming the frontier states of Indiana, Ohio and Illinois. He was a preacher as well as an apple-seed planter.

APPLE-tizing RECIPE BOOKS

Have a few parents of your students bake their favorite apple treat. Ask them to send the recipe to school with the treat. Duplicate the recipes so each child has a copy. Students can then put them into the form of a recipe book.

You can also have an apple tasting party where you cut into bite size samples of the offerings brought by parents.

Johnny Appleseed Puppet

To make your Johnny Appleseed Puppet, fold a sheet of 12" x 18" in thirds lengthwise, then in half. Finally, fold both the top and bottom edges back. (See drawing.) Students can add details with pieces of scrap paper and collage materials.

....students insert hands here!

WAB

APPLE UNSCRAMBLE

Use the apple names from the list at the bottom of the page to help you unscramble the words below. Write the correct spelling next to the scrambled word.

snalsI doeRh gnineerG _____

elDiocisu eRd _____

ppiiPn twoeNn _____

ntieenGvras _____   aStrr _____

Tywtne Oeucn _____   teWalhy _____

elDiocisu loGnde _____   wBniald _____

ppbrCalea _____   aJnohtan _____

ypS nrehtroN _____   MItscnoh _____

tyaSamn _____   eRmo euBayt _____

niseapW _____   mGirse lGdnoe _____

pImalire kYro _____

Yweoll Ttrnaenrsap _____

*** *** *** *** *** *** *** *** *** *** *** *** ***

APPLE NAMES TO CHOOSE FROM: Twenty Ounce   Red Delicious

Jonathan   Rhode Island Greening   Yellow Transparent

McIntosh   Winesap   Rome Beauty   Crabapple   Grimes Golden

Newton Pippin   Northern Spy   Golden Delicious

Stayman   York Imperial   Starr

Wealthy   Baldwin   Gravenstein

A NOT -

Cut...a bunch of stars about 4"x4".

FOR A FUN START TO SOME OF YOUR DAYS......HIDE A YELLOW STAR in your classroom. The child who finds it reads the directions on it and the class participates.

The finder gets to keep the star.

Directions on the star might be: Everybody sing Twinkle! Twinkle! Little Star. OR Let's say the alphabet BACKWARDS!

Count by 10's to 500.

Have a parade around the classroom. Everybody must be a baby kitten.

The star could say......

HUMmmmmm GOOD MORNING TO YOU!

EVERYBODY....WHISTLE A HAPPY TUNE...............

Count by 5's from 100 all the way down to ZERO!

Look out the window and draw two things you see.

Clap your hands two times, turn around twice, sing Happy Birthday(to a famous person whose birthday is that day).

The note on the star says..........

LOOK IN THE CUPBOARD.

A note in the cupboard says...........

OPEN THE BOX NEAR THE RECORD PLAYER.

A note found there says............ENJOY LISTENING TO THIS RECORD.

ON THE STAR COULD BE A RIDDLE .... What has panes but doesn't ache?

What is black and white and red all over? The students have until

noon to form an answer.

Put a little color-fun in those first days of school to ease the children back into the routine of school life! A good way to teach color words also occurs. On a pre-announced special color day, everybody should try to wear clothing of that color. TEACHER SHOULD TOO!

color-'full'

MELLOW YELLOW Find all the yellow pictures in magazines. (Always have magazines handy for cutting and pasting.) Make a collage of these on a big piece of 22" x 28" piece of paper. Tape to the chalkboard. Ditto sheets of activities on yellow paper. Serve lemonade as a special treat.

ON WITH OLD ORANGE!

Draw all the things in the world that are orange. With water colors see how many shades of orange can be created. Each child gets an orange to eat. Peel it! Break it apart! Count the sections! Will the seeds grow? Plant and see!

You will find suggestions for a very special <u>RED</u> day in the September section of this book.

<u>GREEN!</u> <u>GREEN!</u> <u>GREEN!</u> can be found in the March section of.......

<u>Spring Surprises</u>, also published by Good Apple.

<u>BLUE</u>, <u>BLUE</u>, do a blue!

  Make a bluebird of happiness.
 List words and expressions that have
          BLUE in them.
blueberry,true blue, blew, the blues
        DON''T FORGET PERIWINKLE
 Write, paint, color all day in blue.
    .....for a special Blueberries Day.

<u>BOO</u>, <u>BLACK</u> Do some measuring with licorice sticks or lashes. Give each child a 12" x 18" piece of black construction paper. The task is to create a night scene. Students can use chalk or cut and glue construction paper shapes. Make three lists: things that are always black, things that are sometimes black, things that are never black. Bring a blindfold to class. Each child gets ten minutes in the dark. After the ten minutes the child lists things that were heard.

Have a hero day. What is a hero? What characteristics make a person a hero?

Draw a picture of your favorite hero.

Everyone bring something to help fill a hero sandwich. Maybe the school will supply the bread.

Celebrate the Emperor of Japan's birthday. Make him a dragon card. Include social studies, and language arts activities.

HAVE A BACKWARDSSDRAWKCAB DAY.
Write names in reverse.
Sit backwards in seats.
Reverse the daily schedule.

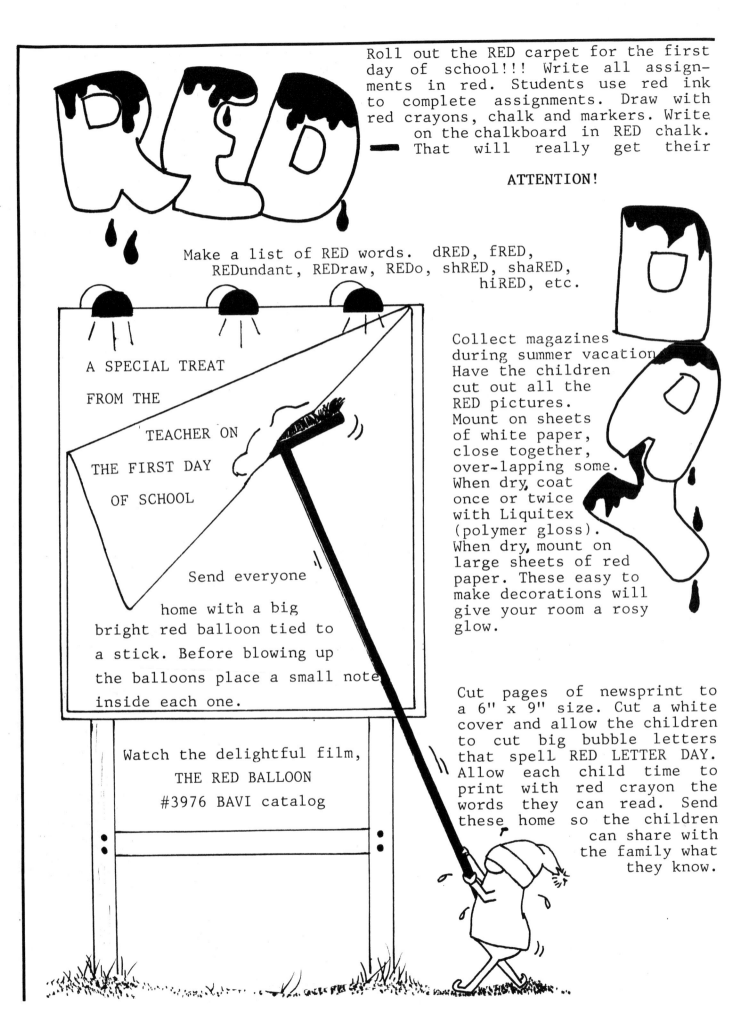

Roll out the RED carpet for the first day of school!!! Write all assignments in red. Students use red ink to complete assignments. Draw with red crayons, chalk and markers. Write on the chalkboard in RED chalk. That will really get their

ATTENTION!

Make a list of RED words. dRED, fRED, REDundant, REDraw, REDo, shRED, shaRED, hiRED, etc.

A SPECIAL TREAT

FROM THE

TEACHER ON

THE FIRST DAY

OF SCHOOL

Send everyone

home with a big bright red balloon tied to a stick. Before blowing up the balloons place a small note inside each one.

Watch the delightful film,
THE RED BALLOON
#3976 BAVI catalog

Collect magazines during summer vacation. Have the children cut out all the RED pictures. Mount on sheets of white paper, close together, over-lapping some. When dry, coat once or twice with Liquitex (polymer gloss). When dry, mount on large sheets of red paper. These easy to make decorations will give your room a rosy glow.

Cut pages of newsprint to a 6" x 9" size. Cut a white cover and allow the children to cut big bubble letters that spell RED LETTER DAY. Allow each child time to print with red crayon the words they can read. Send these home so the children can share with the family what they know.

OOPS!

Make a list of words that
are hues and tints of red.

SCARLET

CRIMSON

CHERRY

On a piece of white construction
paper draw all the things you can
think of that are RED.

Using the rolls of
refrigerator sugar cookie dough, have
the children cut out a big letter "R"
(for red). Then either sprinkle with
red sugar or frost with icing that
has been tinted RED. To make a
pattern for the "R" cut a sturdy
piece of cardboard. Children can
cut around the pattern with a table
knife.

Make a graph showing
who is wearing red.....
socks, shirts, ribbons, pants,
hair.....etc.

Fold a 12" x 18" piece of white paper
in half. Print one one side

WHAT IS!

and on the other side print **WHAT IS NOT!**

The task for each student is to fill
each side with pictures of things that
are or are not RED.

At the end of the day send all of the
RED LETTER DAY activities home.

........then catch their attention throughout the entire year with our offerings (or the following pages) of some lively activities to make drill and the learning of skills enjoyable and challenging.

Some of the ideas/directions presented are similar to those found in Winter Wonders and Spring Surprises but they are favorites of our students and in this book we have adapted them to the fall season.

A camera can be a basic tool of the classroom. If one is present it will be used more than one might think it would. Take pictures occasionally. Send them home with a note saying......CAUGHT YOUR CHILD DOING THIS.

SECRET MESSAGES

From colored construction paper cut pieces a 4" x 6" size. Write a word to be sounded out or a short sentence on the bottom half of each piece. Fold the paper as shown and staple it shut. On the front draw a simple seasonal picture, a leaf, a Pilgrim, an Indian, etc. Pass out the messages and have the students open carefully and read. Store in a small box and use several times.

Title the box.... secret message.

Cover large pin-on buttons with adhesive paper. Put the numeral "1" on two badges, the numeral "2" on two badges, and the numeral "3" on two badges, etc. Pass one badge to each child in the reading group. The teacher spreads some vocabulary words, face up on the floor. The teacher calls out a number and one of the vocabulary words. The two children wearing that number try to be the first to slap the word that has been called.

badge beat

FOR ALL

A BINGO

SEASONS

Draw and duplicate a BING-O matrix. Make a different matrix for each month of the fall season. Write appropriate words on the chalkboard and have the students copy them, placing them at random about the matrix. Laminate for longer use. Store in a box decorated for that month. Each year when the month arrives a game is ready to play.

For September the words for the matrix could include the names of school personnel and:

football   fall   autumn
leaves   frost   welcome
Labor Day   school   September

names of new students.

Mr. Smith	FROST	Labor day	FOOT BALL	Leaves
Veterans DAY	AUTUMN	Don Dieleman	HARVEST	Mrs. Wright
Billy Jones	Color Tops	FREE FALL	Principal Peters	4th GRADE
Holloween	SCHOOL	WORLD SERIES	September	Jane Dougly
Sandy Warren	Columbus Day	JANITOR JOHN	Thanksgiving	WELCOME

Adapt the "OH SHUCKS" game in the Thanksgiving section to a game appropriate for September.

FUN FOLDERS

18"

yellow

8+2=
Name

12"

brown

Staple

trim your door...

If you're tired of having a plain looking classroom door, you might try what two clever teachers down the hall at our school have done to their doors. One has a criss-cross motif. It was done by taping colored roving yarn and adding seasonal decorations in the diamond shaped areas that were created.

The other door, the door to the art room, has curtains made of crepe paper. Small cutouts are taped to the glass. Cutouts and the color of the crepe paper are changed each month.

You will need two seasonal colors of paper. Fold one in half the long way and the other fold in half from top to bottom. The long narrow one will form the pocket of a folder. Staple the pocket on the sides as shown in the illustration. You now have a four pocket storage container. In each section place a worksheet or special activity for the students to try. When the worksheet is completed, decorate the section with a gummed sticker. When all appropriate activities have been completed, send it home.

erase away

transportation
(20)

corral
(7)

manners
(10)

handle
(5)

Very little preparation is needed for this favorite. Write words on the chalkboard that can be sounded out. Make the words as challenging as possible. Give each word a number. Give a low number for the easier words. Higher numbers should be assigned as the words increase in difficulty. Players take turns. Player may choose any word he thinks he can sound out. If correct, the player receives the number of points indicated. Play continues until all words have been pronounced correctly. The player with the most points is the winner. When the word has been correctly pronounced, it can be erased from the chalkboard. Children will choose to play this game often so keep a list of words handy.

mystery words

Fold pieces of paper in half. On the outside flap write the names of the students in a reading group. Inside, print a word for the student to sound out. Place all folded pieces of paper on a table. Call the names of the children one at a time. As his name is called the child selects one of the papers with his name on it. He lifts the flap and tries to pronounce the word. Play continues until each child has had an opportunity to try each of his words.

secret messages

croak

skunk

bus bump

GAME BOX

We keep a prettily covered shoe box at our reading and planning table. Here we store the various reading games. As plans are made, the students choose the games they wish to include in the week's activities. With the game ideas at the student's fingertips, planning time is shortened.

Here is another game for which there are many, many formats.

Format #1 is the more quiet version but still much loved. Make 4 cards per child. The same word should be on all the player's cards. Shuffle all the player's cards and pass them out 4 to a child. The object of the game is to get 4 words that are alike. After the children have their cards in their hands, they pass one card to the right and then reach to take a card from the person to their left. It takes a little work to get the passing going smoothly, but it is worth the effort. Do not allow the students to put a card down for another child. If you do this, there will not be a backlog. The object is not to be fast but to get four word cards that are alike. When someone has 4 alike, he quietly slips a finger to the side of his nose. The last one to catch on is the SKUNK.

Format #2 is similar to the first but, instead of putting a finger to the nose, the winner must snatch one of the objects that have been placed in the center of the playing area. There should be one less objects than children playing the game. The child who does not get an object is the SKUNK.

skunk

STICK A TREAT IN THEIR REPORT CARD....STICK OF GUM, NEW ERASER, PENCIL, PAD OF PAPER

ring around the reading group.

Pass strips of paper around the circle of reading group members. On each paper strip should be a sentence. When a signal is given by the leader, the first child to read his sentence gets a pretzel. Plain drill words may be used instead of a sentence. The signal should be something not too obvious....a wink, a grin, or a tap of a finger.

If the sentences involve following directions (walk to the door and come back whistling), the game is a good reading comprehension activity.

On the following pages you will find several organization sheets to help your year go smoothly. Sheet A: Make one copy for each child. Place all sheets in a notebook. Assess individual progress each month. this provides a neat accurate record. SheetB: A reading plan sheet for each reading group. This helps keep weekly plans organized. SheetC: Place this at the child's desk for open house along with the "All About You" materials from the You-nique section. Sheet D: Show this basic concepts sheet at conference time. It is a good way to report progress to parents. It can be updated periodically.

things to do.....	MONDAY	TUESDAY	WEDNESDAY	THURSDAY	FRIDAY
Workbook					
Read					
Something Special					
New Words					

This is where I sit!

Name

I'm so proud!

I'm in first grade!

Ask me to read these words.

Reading						
Workbook						
Math						
Writing						
Problems						
Successes						

A.

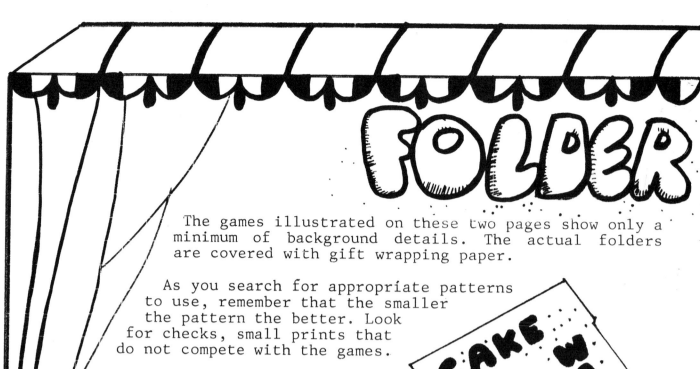

FOLDER

The games illustrated on these two pages show only a minimum of background details. The actual folders are covered with gift wrapping paper.

As you search for appropriate patterns to use, remember that the smaller the pattern the better. Look for checks, small prints that do not compete with the games.

The designs on the gift wrap will also help you come up with themes for the games.

CAKE WALK: Each child rolls a die, in turn, picks a yellow card, reads it and moves that many spaces. If the child should land on a green or orange space, he must take a card from that pile and do what it says. The yellow cards may be for normal vocabulary (or math) skills. The green and orange cards will have either very hard questions or ask the drawer to complete a task. For example: Go to the door, open and close it three times.

FAIR

The ZOOM game will teach any basic vocabulary words that you wish to emphasize. Place word cards face down. Players draw alternately and move the number of spaces that you have marked in the corner of each card. The easier the word the smaller the number should be.

If the player does not know the word, he may not move.

For this game you might like to use the names of animals and the sounds that they make. For older students use some of the Latin genus names of the animals.

elephant (loxodonta)

lion (felis leo)

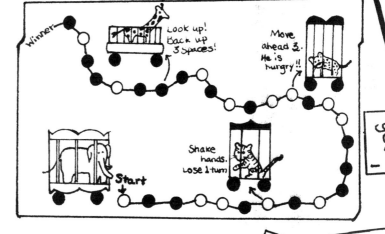

POCKET PATCH

Children are to take the strips and place them in the proper pocket. Change the nouns on the pockets to seasons, countries, animals or products, animals, words or holidays of a country.

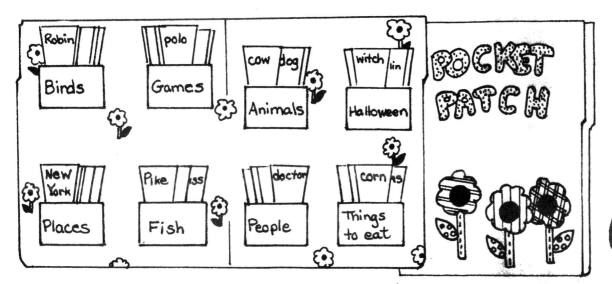

COVER UP!

Two children can play. You will need one stack of yellow cards and one stack of white cards. Each child takes one of the stacks of cards and places them face down in front of him. In turn, the players draw a card and place it correctly over the proper sound. In this game we are only concerned that the player hears the proper sound. For example, "ou" or "ow" can be covered with either cloud or shower. After all spaces have been covered, the player whose color of card shows the most on the gameboard is the winner.

After the initial sound has been covered there is no peeking to see under the words.

What should be taught
is what the sound says
in the square, and then as the words
cover the sounds, what those sounds
say within the word.

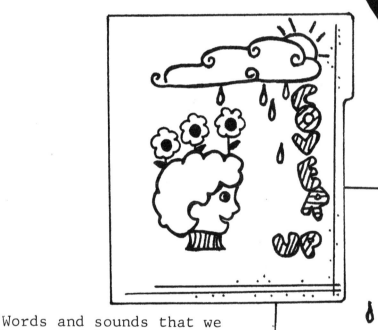

ōw	ar	aw	ing
ee	oy	ou	oa
oi	ar	ie	ight
ai	ur	oo	aw

Words and sounds that we
have used include:

ow   bow, tow, bowl, grow,
    boat, mower

ou cloud, proud, about, shout,
    pout, doubt, cow, now,
    towel, shower, tower

oi, oy boil, soil, foil,
    broil, coil, toy, boy

ar bark, part, shark, dark, mark, carton, market

ight bright, light, sight, kits, mighty, bite, quite, white

    ur burn, teacher, water, furnace, squirt, dirt, turtle

OTHER SOUNDS TO USE: aw, oo, ee, oa, ai, and ie

Parent-school conferences are a MUST in any school's plan for education. These meetings are a rewarding device to further communications between parent and school. Problems can be presented and discussed. Both parents and teachers want to share feelings about the child's progress.

BUT DON'T FORGET THE CHILD!

Both of us like to share with the child what we will be discussing with his/her parents.

A CHILD-MADE BOOKLET FOR CONFERENCES!

Illustrated below are pages for a conference booklet that we have found to be very useful. The cover of the booklet is designed by the child. When completed, the booklet is shown first to the child and then to parents.

Attitudes

1. The behavior/attitude of _____ is usually:
   _____

2. Health/social behaviors that need attention include
   _____

3. Work habits that are shown:
   _____

↕ 8¼"

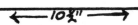
← 10½" →

Skills

READING

Attitude toward reading _____
_____

Mastery of vocabulary _____
_____

Independent activities _____
_____

Problems you could help with __
_____

MATH

Ability to make numerals accurately _____
_____

Understanding of basic concepts _____
_____

Work on daily mastery sheets ___
_____

Mom and Dad

Favorite activities at home include _____
_____

Responsibilities at home are:
_____

Attitude toward school is: ____
_____

Special help child needs at school _____

Save the boxes that ditto masters come in or locate others of a similar size. Cover the tops with contact paper. Label the ends of the boxes with the names of the months of the school year. As you come across a good idea, worksheet, recipe or project suitable for your students, tuck it away in the appropriate box. A quick check at the beginning of each month will be a good reminder of ideas that are available.

Teacher Tips

Postcards of Praise

At the beginning of each year, invest in a stack of postcards. Address one (NOW, while you are thinking of it!) to each student in your class. Whenever a youngster achieves a goal or has worked consistently well, note it with pride on the postcard and drop it in the mail. Everyone from the mailman to the parent will be aware of the child's success. AND you have communicated with each child in a positive way.

Enlarge this ketchup bottle for use as a signal for students that today is KETCH-UP DAY. All corrections, incomplete work should be finished before the final bell rings for the day. If you hang the bottle on the door before the children arrive, all will know what day it is when they enter the classroom.

Teacher Planning Sheet

Duplicate a dozen copies of the sheet on the next page and store them in the back cover of your lesson plan book. The next time you're ready to plan a science or social studies unit, you'll be able to focus on your goal clearly with the help of the sheet. As the unit progresses, note successes and failures and file along with the unit plans. Use as a guide the next time the unit is taught.

Teacher Planning Sheet

major concepts	vocabulary	games, projects & art activities
		audio-visual materials
field trips & speakers	books	

This inventory math sheet can be used as a report card supplement. You can make it any size you want, but a size consistent with your report card would be most appropriate. We've used it in parent-teacher conferences to show parents how their children are progressing. As each child masters one of the tests, a check mark is made beside the task definition. For your covenience we suggest that you construct your own little tests to measure each of the tasks; then ditto them and store each task in a separate folder.

Name _____	Mastery ✓		Mastery ✓
Count to 50 or 100		Add across 1+4+2= Add in a column	
Addition facts 0-5		Tens and ones	
Addition facts 5-10		Money value: penny nickel dime quarter	
Subtraction facts 0-5		Fractions $\frac{1}{2}$ $\frac{1}{4}$ 1/3	
Subtraction facts 5-10		Clocks $\frac{1}{2}$ hour 1 hour	
Greater than, Less than		Subtraction facts 10-20	
Write and count by 2's		Measurement	
Write and count by 5's		Liquid measurement	

Do you get tired of spelling words? Try this....

Cut 9½" x 22" lengths of tagboard and bend the corners over the top of the hanger; then staple. Make one chart for each letter of the alphabet plus some of the blends. Start by printing some of the most often used words on each chart and then add words as children ask for them. When a child asks for a word, ask him what it begins with; then get the chart he directs you to and simply point out the word. As children become more proficient, they will be able to find the charts by themselves. You can even have them alphabetize the charts. They also can be stored conveniently by hanging them on your chalk tray.

OCTOBER

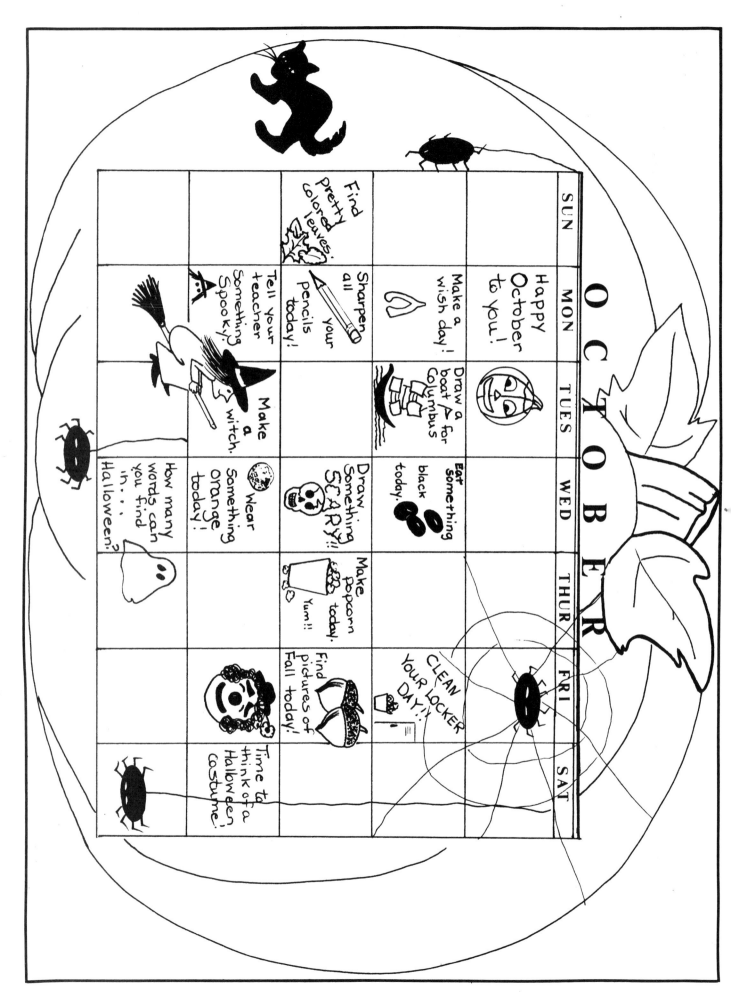

OCTOBER

SUN	MON	TUES	WED	THUR	FRI	SAT
	Happy October to you!	Eat something black today.				
Find pretty colored leaves!	Make a wish day!	Draw a boat for Columbus.	Draw something SCARY!!	Make popcorn today. Yum!!	CLEAN YOUR LOCKER DAY!!	Time to think of a Halloween costume.
Sharpen all your Pencils today!	Make a witch.	Wear something orange today!	Find pictures of Fall today!			
Tell your teacher something Spooky!	How many words can you find in... Halloween?					

Begin with fresh mushrooms to taste from the store, those should be the ONLY fresh ones they eat!

MUSHROOM MEADOW

A cool damp day in autumn is the perfect time to discover mushrooms. You can tie the discovery in with your study of Halloween by adding some science with some superstition. You can begin with a trip to the library in your building. Check for any books, prints, filmstrips or tapes dealing with ....

..SCIENCE and SUPERSTITION......

You can set up this small center inside a cupboard or on a bookshelf where there is very little light, thus simulating the environment of the growth of mushrooms. Arrange a small lamp inside your cupboard to call attention to the activity. Begin with a log--perhaps one you've found in the woods or one you have stacked in your woodpile at home. Using the paper patterns found on the next page, make mushroom task cards and stick them around the edge of the log with double-stick tape or place them in slits you've cut in the log. Ideas for task sheets and student guides are found on the next page.

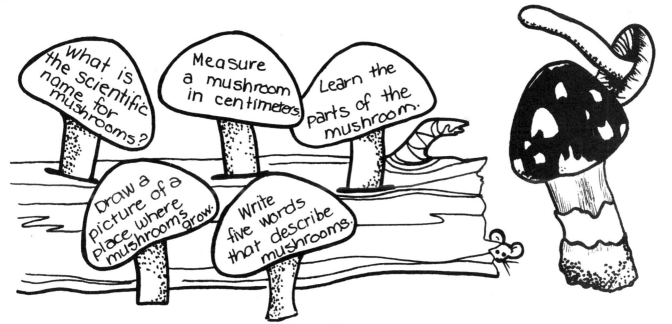

Find the two little mushroom worksheets and use the books you've
checked out to find the information
you need.

pattern

make a
spore print!

MUSHROOM
MEADOW
TASKS

pattern

Using the dictionary, find out the meaning of each of these words: fungi, para-
site, gills, amanita, champignon, myce-
lium, toadstool, chlorophyll, sporophore
and agarics.

pattern

List those
mushrooms that
are poisonous.

Make a list of at least eight kinds
of poisonous mushrooms and eight
kinds of edible mushrooms. Then
draw pictures of four kinds of each
and label them.

What are shelf mushrooms? Draw a
picture of one. Find out if you
can safely eat shelf mushrooms.

Write a story called "The Magic
Mushroom." Use the mushroom paper
for your story.

Using the mushrooms with word pieces
on them, make a list of all the
words you can make with those pieces.

MUSHROOM MEADOW

Spore Prints

To make a spore print you will need a fresh mushroom, a piece of dark paper and a jar that will fit over the paper. Place the mushroom, gills down, on the paper. Cover the jar and wait patiently for two days. Then lift the jar carefully off the top of the mushroom and remove the cap carefully. You should see a lovely pattern on the paper that has been made by the spores that have fallen off. Spray with acrylic lacquer to preserve the pattern. Are all the spores the same color?

Mixed Mushrooms

Cut a stack of paper mushrooms and place one of the word pieces below on each of the mushrooms. Students then use the word pieces to form new words. Have them work in teams to see who can make the most words.

al oi au ou ea oo ee
ui ie y oa gl gr j k
l m spr sp st sp sn
sm scr tr th sw wh ik
il lp lt m mb mp n ng
nk rp th ss st sk sh
ed er est ful ing ly
able s es less...

are some word parts you can use...

ful

Magic Mushroom

Cut paper mushrooms out of tan or gray construction paper and label each "The Magic Mushroom." Assign each student the task of writing a story that goes with the title. Then hang them on the bulletin board for others to read.

Label the parts of a mushroom

cap
cup
gill
stem
ring

CUT HERE

Shapely Question

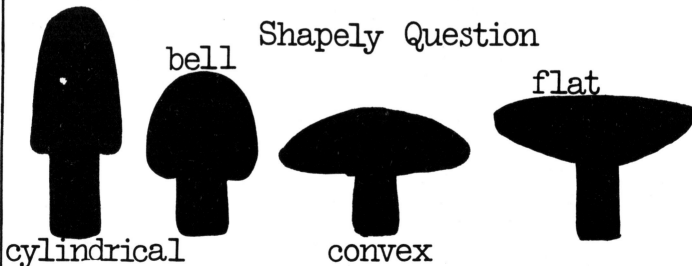

bell

flat

cylindrical

convex

Mushrooms fall into various groups which you can determine by looking at the shapes of the mushrooms themselves. Find out the names of two mushrooms for each shape you see above and write the names of those mushrooms under the shapes.

Patches of Autumn

Collect books and poems from your library and start each day with a few paragraphs or lines from a good wordsmith. File them in a recipe box with monthly dividers for finger-tip poetry ready to read at the beginning of each day.

...on a table

Gather several boxes of bricks and arrange them in a stepping-stone fashion. Cover with a piece of autumn-colored fabric. Add a vase of milkweed pods and ask your kids to bring in "autumn treasures" of their own (fall flowers, nuts, gourds, weeds, etc.). When your display is complete, make up a list of the dominating colors; then paint one of the items in still life as an art project. You could also develop a descriptive writing assignment using the adjectives associated with autumn.

....at the easel

At the easel in your classroom provide only autumn colors for students to use to sponge paint leaf-shaped pieces of paper. Leaves can also be cut of only autumn colors. You might wish to create a bulletin board for the classroom or create covers for books of the writing assignments that the students complete. Brown wrapping paper is nice to use for this project and it is fairly inexpensive.

.....around the corner

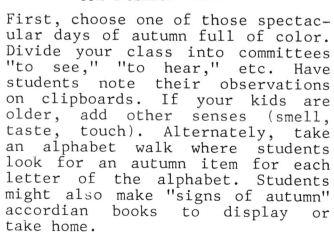

First, choose one of those spectacular days of autumn full of color. Divide your class into committees "to see," "to hear," etc. Have students note their observations on clipboards. If your kids are older, add other senses (smell, taste, touch). Alternately, take an alphabet walk where students look for an autumn item for each letter of the alphabet. Students might also make "signs of autumn" accordian books to display or take home.

Patches of Autumn from

Your students can make colored dyes from autumn leaves with the help of hands to crunch and several bottles of alcohol. First, have children gather lots of autumn leaves and sort them by color. Covering the surface with newspaper, have children

alcohol

crunch their leaves into very small pieces and put them in glass jars. Direct them to use a different jar for each leaf color. Then pour alcohol over the top of the leaves. Allow some of the alcohol to evaporate and cover the jar overnight. When the color has been drawn from the leaves, remove the leaves. Have students dip small pieces of cloth into the dye. Long thin strips make perfect bookmarks and the more square pieces make good backgrounds for autumn pictures. Have students add finishing touches by using fine line markers, stitchery or fabric crayons. The cloth can be mounted onto construction paper and used also as cards. Finally, spray sizing on the cloth to make it stiffer and easier to work with.

a Mother Nature original

autumn leaf juice

a plot of dirt

Autumn is the time of year to plant for "spring surprises." Send a note home asking parents to send a few tulip or daffodil bulbs left over from their fall planting. Select a favorite spot in the school yard--perhaps under your window--for your planting. Pick one of those beautiful fall afternoons for your planting and be certain to make the hole for each bulb one and one-half times the length of the bulb. If your school yard doesn't lend itself to gardening, ask for a volunteer yard nearby. The walk will make a nice field trip for your students.

weeds & seeds

Celebrate seeds by gathering them in a nearby forest or field. Have students bring Dad's oldest, wooliest and seed-catchingest jacket or shirt. A wooly pair of old mittens or wool socks over the shoes will also serve the purpose as an excellent seed catcher. Have your students walk through the seedy patch or field brushing and bumping against anything that grows. Upon your return to the classroom, have your kids pick off as many seeds as possible for identification. You might also try dragging a rope tied to an old sock through the field as a method of collecting seeds.

Cut a giant leaf from a piece of brown butcher paper. Have your students cover the leaf with "color" words that describe autumn. Encourage the students to create a list of at least 75 words. Give praise when words like brass, auburn, rust, bittersweet and walnut are contributed.

Patches

of

Autumn

Use one of your bulletin boards as a billboard. Cover it with plain white paper and add black half circles as shown. Label it "Autumn Billboard." As you travel through your study of autumn, have children add signs of autumn to the billboard in the media of their choice. As you read stories or show filmstrips, after walks or talks with your kids, have them add their observations to the billboard. Don't forget to include things like frogs hibernating in the mud, squirrels tucking away their acorns and wooly creatures.

on a billboard

What things FALL? Cut a giant autumn leaf or acorn. Use it to collect the names of things that fall.-Like leaves, children, apples . . . .

in a box

Get a nice big cardboard box and select an environment to display as an autumn diorama. Divide students into teams to perform various tasks on the project. Have them collect collage materials and use scrap construction paper to make the items used in the diorama. Gather additional boxes and have the students make similar scenes for the other seasons. Stack the boxes in totem pole fashion.

capitalize...

You can make your own "cow town" by covering a low table with something that looks like a horse blanket. Find some split rails (You might try borrowing them from a local lumber yard.) and build a small corral to fence in your "range." Add a few bales of hay for atmosphere. Bring in as many horse related items as you can. Saddle, bridle, reins, saddle blanket, and pans of different kinds of horse feed are good examples. You can also draw pictures of them on a ditto and distribute them to smaller children for coloring and labeling. These will make excellent additions to their WILD WEST folders. You might even tell stories around a cracker barrel; and to add real flavor, pass out real crackers.

Ask someone with some "horse sense" (expertise) to come to your classroom and give a talk. Encourage the visitor to display some items and answer the many questions that will be asked.

Don't forget to give your corral a name. Examples are CACTUS JUNCTION, ONE HORSE TOWN and simply COW TOWN; however, it's more fun to create your own name. Those of you who live in the real WEST should do an excellent job with this center.

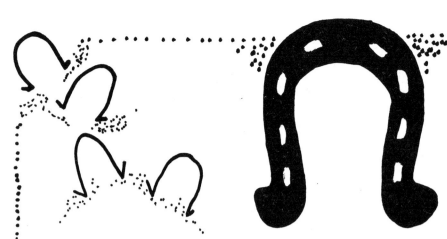

Hang a "good luck" horseshoe over your door and have your students make smaller versions for use on their lockers.

Challenge your cowboys and cowbelles to find as many words as they can that begin with the word <u>horse</u>. Examples are horseback, horse chestnut, horsehair, horse<u>fly</u>, horseradish, horseplay, horse pistol, horsepower, horselaugh, horsetail and horsey.

Have the children draw all kinds of horses. Make them galloping, rearing, pulling a wagon, etc. Find as many names of horses as you can.

Write to a nearby race track for pictures or literature you could use in your WILD WEST center.

Decorate front with bubble letters.

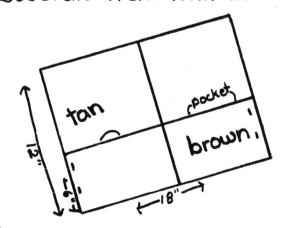

tan
pocket
brown
12"
18"

Here is a popular folder fun idea in which children will keep all their WILD WEST papers. You can let them take the folders home to show their parents at the end of the unit study.

"WILD WEST" folder
pockets form on both back and front!

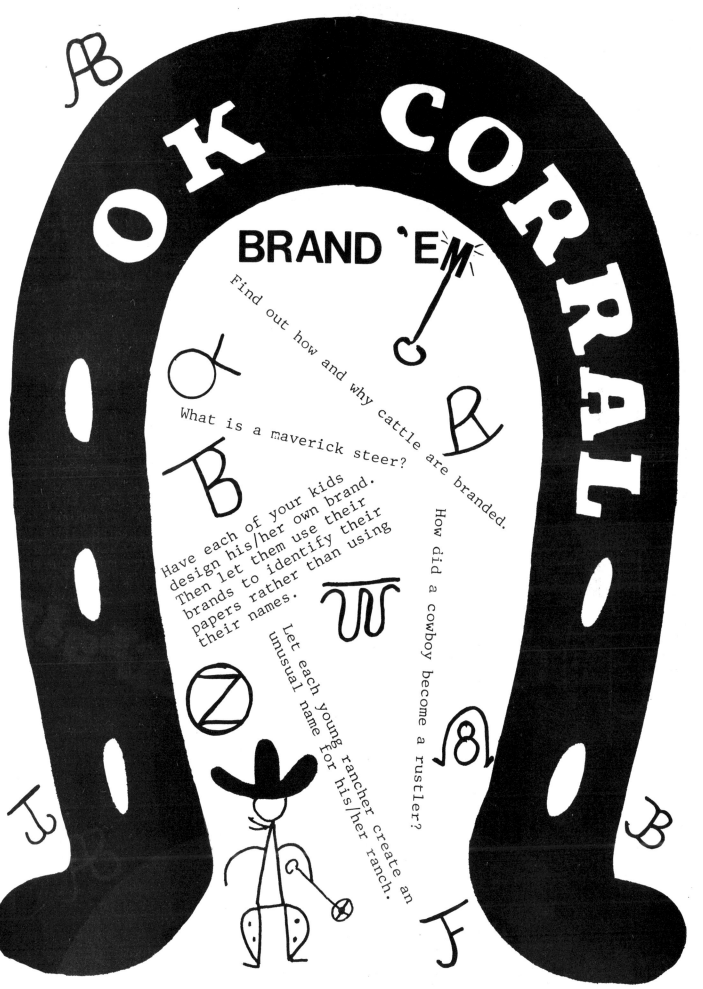

OK CORRAL

BRAND 'EM

Find out how and why cattle are branded.

What is a maverick steer?

Have each of your kids design his/her own brand. Then let them use their brands to identify their papers rather than using their names.

How did a cowboy become a rustler?

Let each young rancher create an unusual name for his/her ranch.

Here's another folder fun game. The object is to teach upper and lower case letters.

Children take turns drawing cards. If a player finds a match on his boot, he puts a colored disc over it. The first player to completely cover his boot or hat wins the game. Be certain to make duplicate letters so there are extra pieces.

hook 'em...

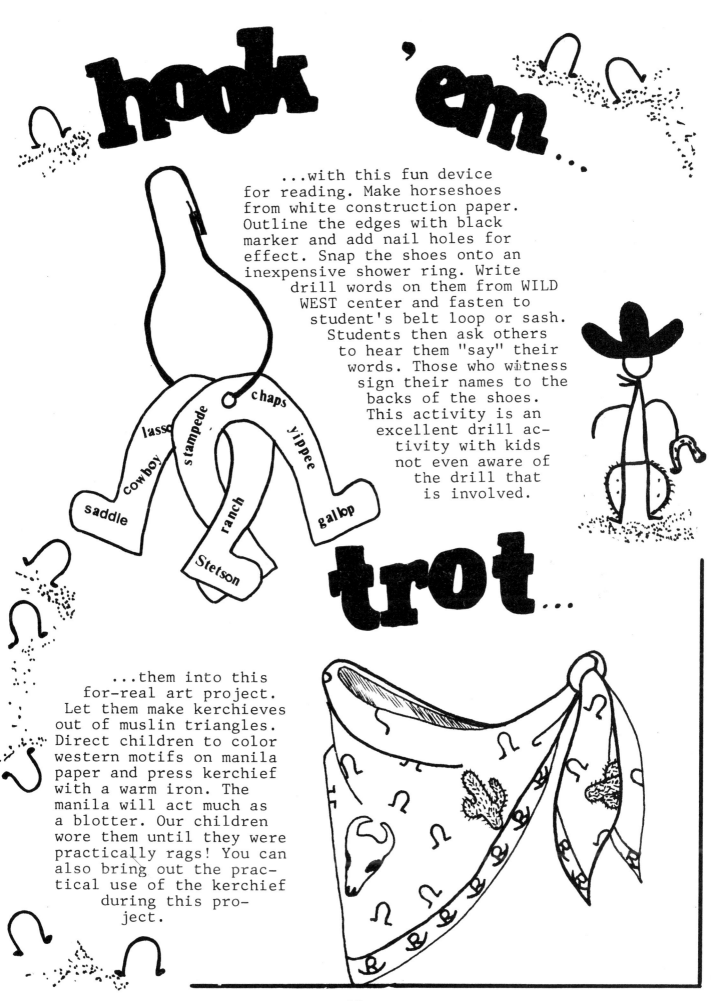

...with this fun device for reading. Make horseshoes from white construction paper. Outline the edges with black marker and add nail holes for effect. Snap the shoes onto an inexpensive shower ring. Write drill words on them from WILD WEST center and fasten to student's belt loop or sash. Students then ask others to hear them "say" their words. Those who witness sign their names to the backs of the shoes. This activity is an excellent drill activity with kids not even aware of the drill that is involved.

lasso
stampede
chaps
cowboy
yippee
saddle
ranch
gallop
Stetson

trot...

...them into this for-real art project. Let them make kerchieves out of muslin triangles. Direct children to color western motifs on manila paper and press kerchief with a warm iron. The manila will act much as a blotter. Our children wore them until they were practically rags! You can also bring out the practical use of the kerchief during this project.

Country Music

We can't forget the "lull-abies" the cowboys would sing at night to quiet their herds. Many of these songs were sad and melancholy. Teach some of these songs to your class or ask for help from the music department. It is preferable to get someone who can play the guitar to add to the effect of the campfire-type atmosphere. If you have trouble finding songs, look to your library for western or folk songs of early Americana.

I live in

...in reading class by making this hombre about a 9" x 12" size through the use of an opaque projector. Make each of these parts out of railroad board, cut and laminate: arms, legs, face, pants, shirt, and boots. Make 2" x 3" cards with practice words on them and print a number on each one. The numbers will correspond to the appropriate body parts that are to be added to make up the "whole" cowboy. The first to complete his cowboy wins. Use this key:
#1-pants...#2-shirt...#3-arms
#4-face...#5-hat...#6-boots
Put these directions on the inside cover of the box that holds the cards and decorate with a western motif. Make three or four cowboys so that several children can play the game.

git along

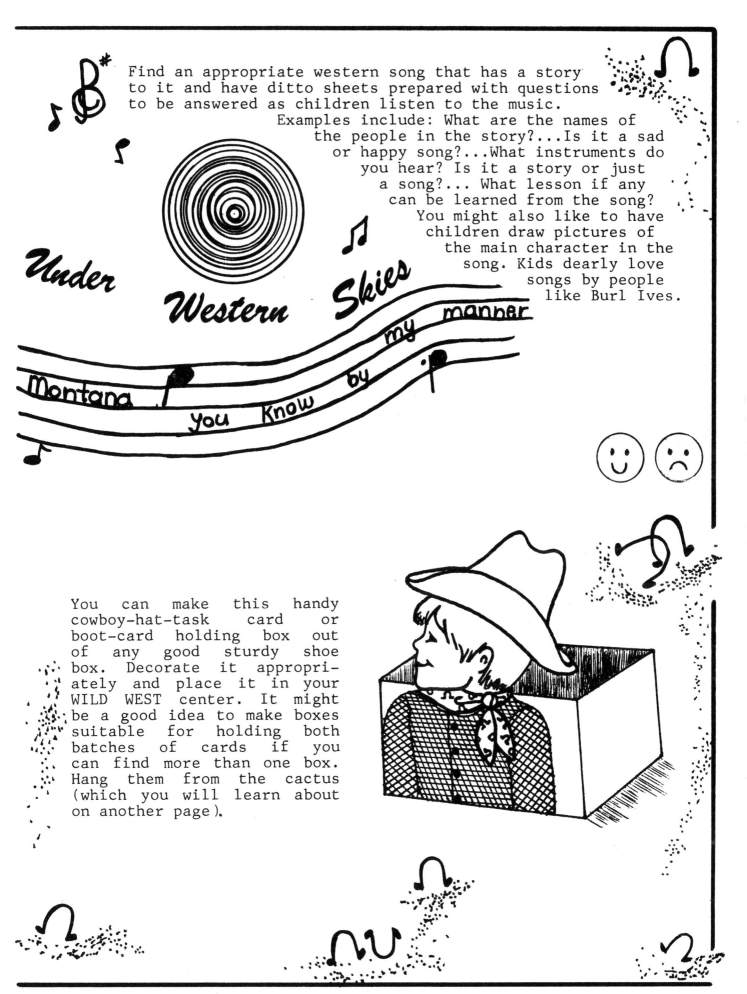

Find an appropriate western song that has a story to it and have ditto sheets prepared with questions to be answered as children listen to the music.

Examples include: What are the names of the people in the story?...Is it a sad or happy song?...What instruments do you hear? Is it a story or just a song?... What lesson if any can be learned from the song? You might also like to have children draw pictures of the main character in the song. Kids dearly love songs by people like Burl Ives.

Under Western Skies

Montana you know by my manner

You can make this handy cowboy-hat-task card or boot-card holding box out of any good sturdy shoe box. Decorate it appropriately and place it in your WILD WEST center. It might be a good idea to make boxes suitable for holding both batches of cards if you can find more than one box. Hang them from the cactus (which you will learn about on another page).

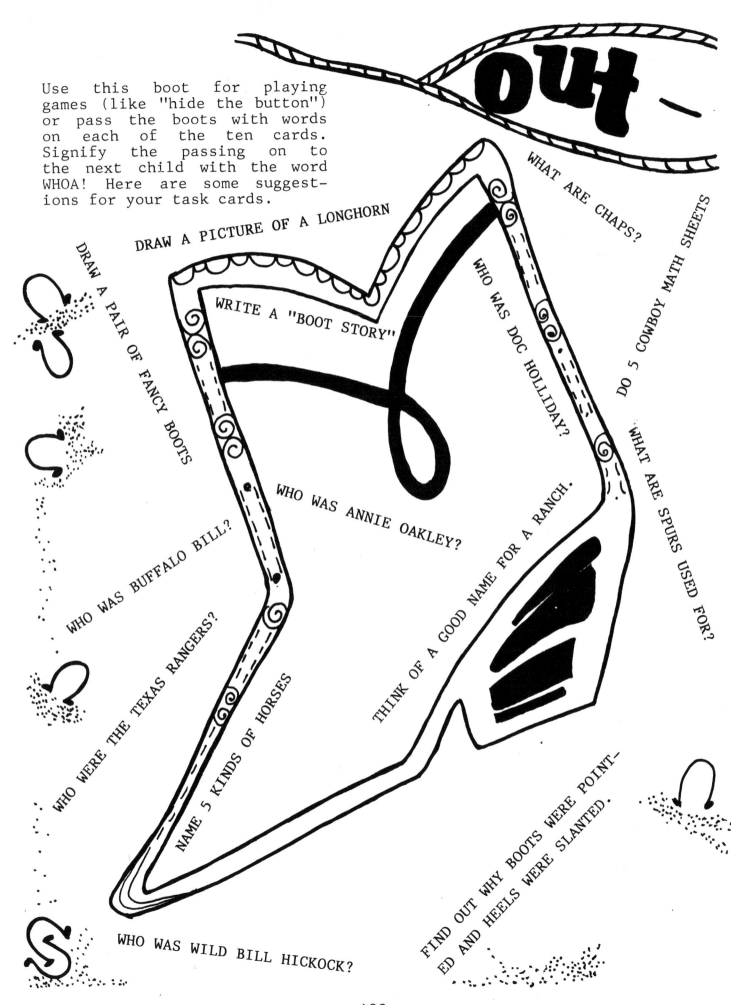

Use this boot for playing games (like "hide the button") or pass the boots with words on each of the ten cards. Signify the passing on to the next child with the word WHOA! Here are some suggestions for your task cards.

OUT—

DRAW A PICTURE OF A LONGHORN

WHAT ARE CHAPS?

DO 5 COWBOY MATH SHEETS

DRAW A PAIR OF FANCY BOOTS

WRITE A "BOOT STORY"

WHO WAS DOC HOLLIDAY?

WHAT ARE SPURS USED FOR?

WHO WAS ANNIE OAKLEY?

WHO WAS BUFFALO BILL?

THINK OF A GOOD NAME FOR A RANCH.

WHO WERE THE TEXAS RANGERS?

NAME 5 KINDS OF HORSES

FIND OUT WHY BOOTS WERE POINT-ED AND HEELS WERE SLANTED.

WHO WAS WILD BILL HICKOCK?

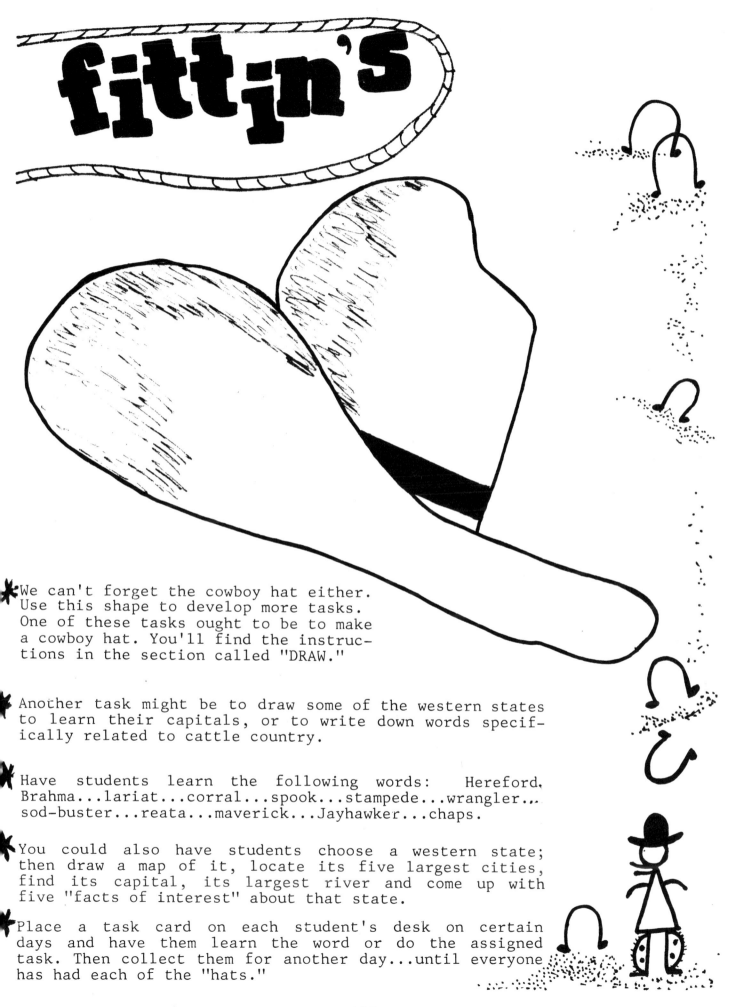

fittin's

We can't forget the cowboy hat either.
Use this shape to develop more tasks.
One of these tasks ought to be to make
a cowboy hat. You'll find the instructions in the section called "DRAW."

Another task might be to draw some of the western states
to learn their capitals, or to write down words specif-
ically related to cattle country.

Have students learn the following words: Hereford,
Brahma...lariat...corral...spook...stampede...wrangler...
sod-buster...reata...maverick...Jayhawker...chaps.

You could also have students choose a western state;
then draw a map of it, locate its five largest cities,
find its capital, its largest river and come up with
five "facts of interest" about that state.

Place a task card on each student's desk on certain
days and have them learn the word or do the assigned
task. Then collect them for another day...until everyone
has had each of the "hats."

git 'em up!

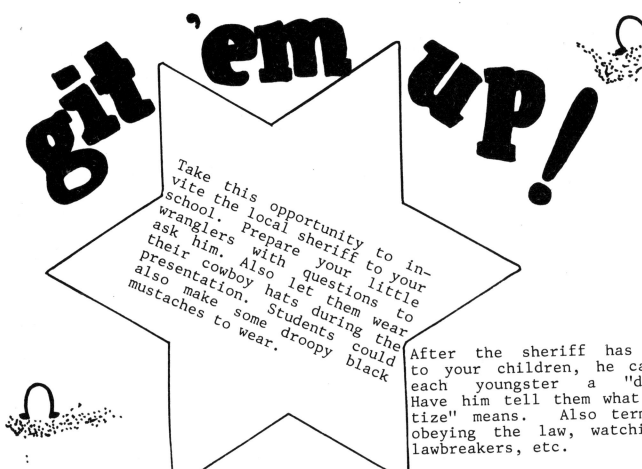

Take this opportunity to invite the local sheriff to your school. Prepare your little wranglers with questions to ask him. Also let them wear their cowboy hats during the presentation. Students could also make some droopy black mustaches to wear.

After the sheriff has talked to your children, he can make each youngster a "deputy." Have him tell them what "deputize" means. Also terms like obeying the law, watching for lawbreakers, etc.

Your students can also draw a picture of an "old-time" sheriff and then one of the sheriff who paid your class a visit. Put them on a 12" x 18" sheet of paper...to the left, the sheriff of yesteryear...to the right, today's sheriff.

QUESTIONS TO ASK YOUR LOCAL SHERIFF

How did you get to be sheriff?
What do you do as sheriff?
Are the things you do today the same as sheriffs of 100 years ago?

Here are some very fine books for this unit. They will help you to find the information you will need to help children develop a center on the WILD WEST.

THE COWBOY TRADE
    Glen Richards
    Holiday House

COWBOYS AND CATTLE COUNTRY
    Irene Swinburne
    Parent's Magazine

COWBOYS: WHAT DO THEY DO?
    Carla Greene
    Harper Row

THE COWBOY BOOK
    Mel Crawford
    Golden Press

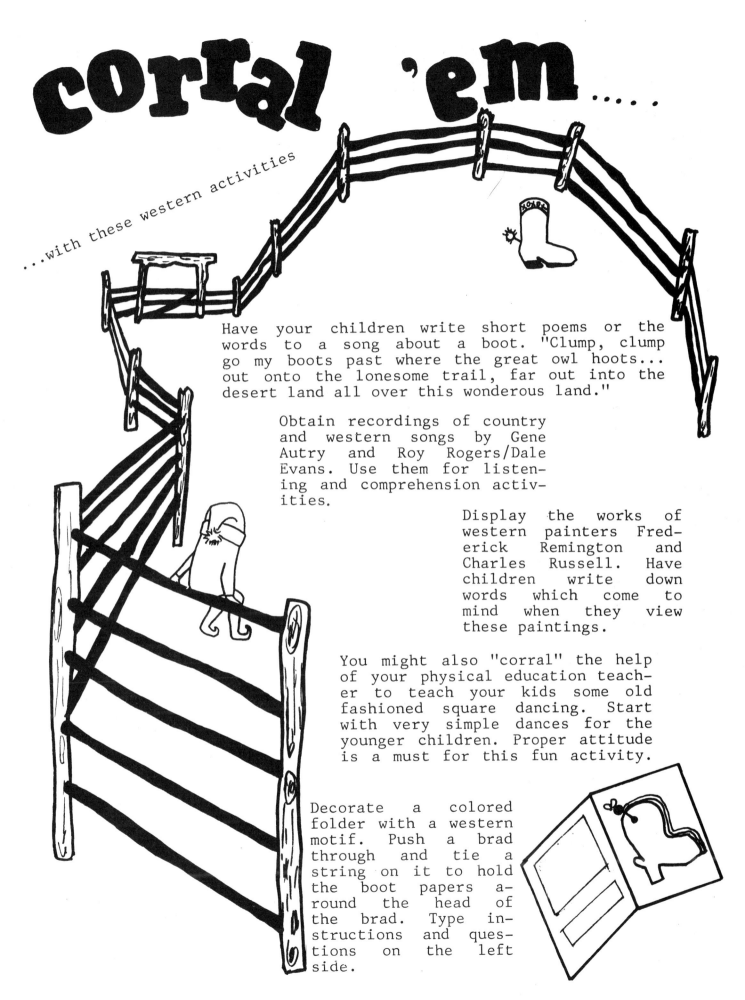

corral 'em....

...with these western activities

Have your children write short poems or the words to a song about a boot. "Clump, clump go my boots past where the great owl hoots... out onto the lonesome trail, far out into the desert land all over this wonderous land."

Obtain recordings of country and western songs by Gene Autry and Roy Rogers/Dale Evans. Use them for listening and comprehension activities.

Display the works of western painters Frederick Remington and Charles Russell. Have children write down words which come to mind when they view these paintings.

You might also "corral" the help of your physical education teacher to teach your kids some old fashioned square dancing. Start with very simple dances for the younger children. Proper attitude is a must for this fun activity.

Decorate a colored folder with a western motif. Push a brad through and tie a string on it to hold the boot papers around the head of the brad. Type instructions and questions on the left side.

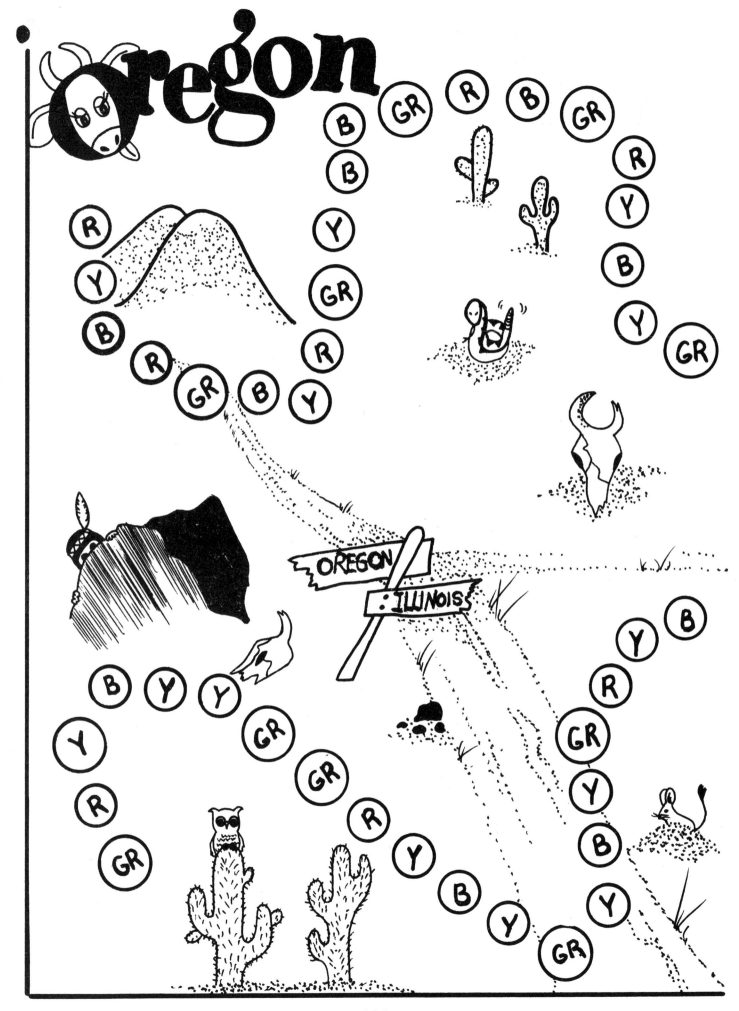

Trail

Directions on next page→

Oregon Trail

directions

Construct this game on a 22" x 28" piece of tagboard. The circles are large and small gummed circles. You can find pictures from old books or magazines to make the board more attractive. Print cards with single words or questions on them. You should also indicate the number of spaces to be moved on each card. Examples of questions: What is a mustang? Who was Geronimo? Define trail wrangler. What is a foxfire? Define stampede. What is a cow lullaby? Name one desert animal. Name the capital of Nevada. TO PLAY THE GAME: Make a card indicating these point values: GREEN +10; YELLOW -5; RED +10; BLUE -5. Give each little "pioneer" 10 counters. Any kind of small token will serve the purpose. Players roll the die to determine order of play. The first player draws a card and answers the question. If he is correct, he moves the indicated number of spaces and collects or gives up the number of counters indicated by the color he lands on. The first to Oregon stops the game and that player with the highest number of counters wins the game.

Horseshoe deal

Yellowstone trail ranch steer cattle foxfire lasso Montana Pike's Peak Reno mustang

Construct this gameboard from a 36" x 36" piece of tagboard. Tack with a loop of tape behind word cards so that you can change cards often. Print on cards words, cities or capitals. The horseshoes are made from black tagboard. Glue washers to one side to add weight.

The first player tosses the shoe and must correctly pronounce the word or respond correctly to the card in order to get the indicated number of points. The first player to accumulate 50 points is the winner.

A variation of this game could include questions or tasks rather than merely words.

WANTED

by

foreman...at the

Print these posters on bright yellow
paper; then burn the edges with a can-
dle to an antique flavor. Use these
for "special assignment" tasks you
give to your students. For example,
you might need a wrangler to be your special
helper...or a cook to handle treats for your
room...or a sheriff to keep law and order
in your room...or a trail boss to organize
an activity. Assign certain qualifications for each
job. Be certain to qualify some of your more "difficult" learners, too. As students complete their "jobs,"
they get to keep the poster, so make plenty.

TOP JOB
ranch

J Bauman
Zinkgraf

Tape out the directions so you can Xerox and ditto
this poster. Also, tape out the word foreman so
you can print in the job you are offering in each
individual situation.

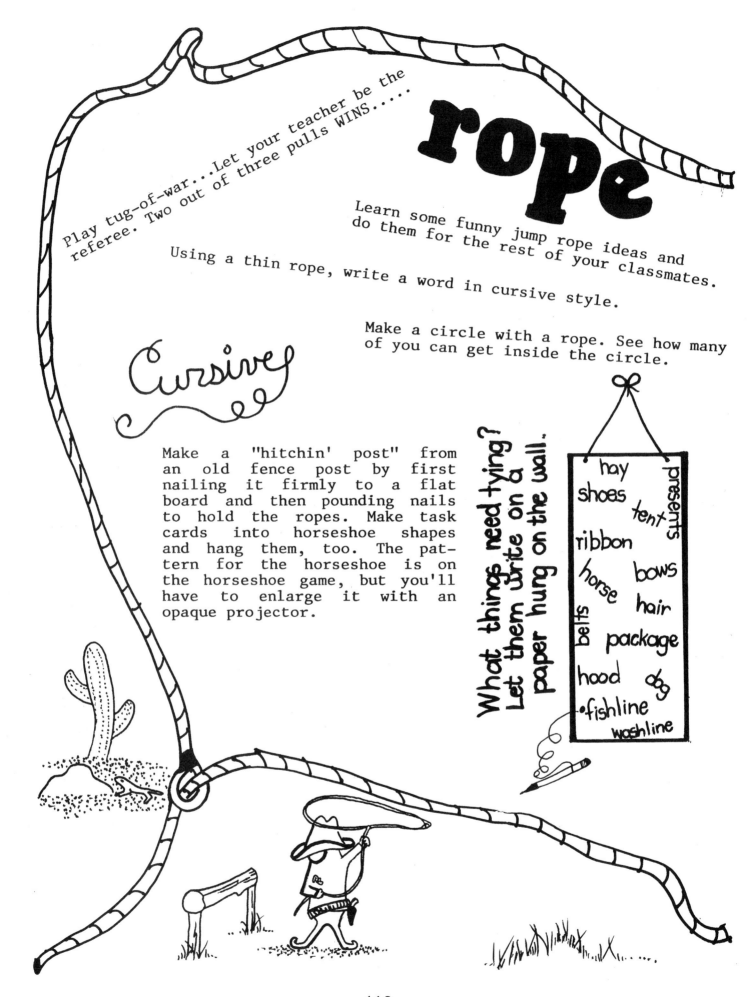

rope

Play tug-of-war...Let your teacher be the referee. Two out of three pulls WINS.....

Learn some funny jump rope ideas and do them for the rest of your classmates.

Using a thin rope, write a word in cursive style.

Make a circle with a rope. See how many of you can get inside the circle.

Cursive

Make a "hitchin' post" from an old fence post by first nailing it firmly to a flat board and then pounding nails to hold the ropes. Make task cards into horseshoe shapes and hang them, too. The pattern for the horseshoe is on the horseshoe game, but you'll have to enlarge it with an opaque projector.

What things need tying? Let them write on a paper hung on the wall.

hay
presents
shoes
tent
ribbon
bows
horse
hair
belts
package
hood
dog
•fishline
washline

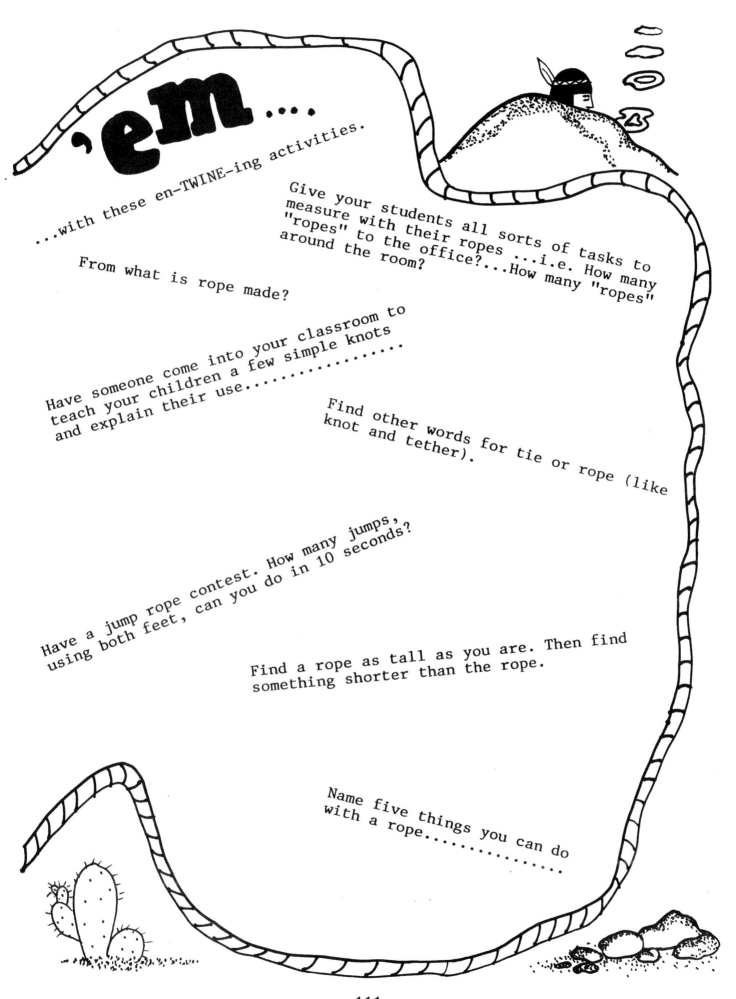

'em ...

...with these en-TWINE-ing activities.

Give your students all sorts of tasks to measure with their ropes ...i.e. How many "ropes" to the office?...How many "ropes" around the room?

From what is rope made?

Have someone come into your classroom to teach your children a few simple knots and explain their use...............

Find other words for tie or rope (like knot and tether).

Have a jump rope contest. How many jumps, using both feet, can you do in 10 seconds?

Find a rope as tall as you are. Then find something shorter than the rope.

Name five things you can do with a rope................

WILD

These hardworking mules are a must in the West. Make this little burro by folding a piece of paper in half; then cutting the shape. The fold will serve as his back.

Mold this buckin' bronco out of brown modeling clay. Or you could use the kind of clay that can be glazed and fired for a lasting souvenir of the WILD WEST.

Make a diorama in a shoe box. Use real sand and rocks......

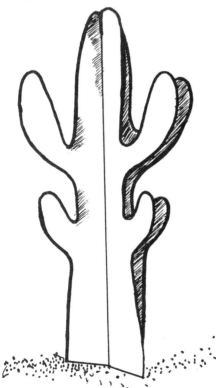

Add to your western theme with these "care-free" cacti. To make them, use railroad board for strength, and cut two of them 7½" tall with a base of 1½". Slit one up from the bottom, the other down from the top. Slide the two together and tape to desks. Add detail with magic markers.

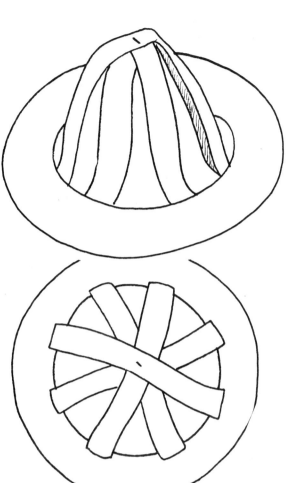

You can make this Stetson out of a 12" circle of brown construction paper. Cut the inner circle to fit the child's head. Three strips of 1" x 14" x 16" can be pasted together to form the crown. Bend the sides up after the crown pieces have dried. A head band can also be added.

Follow the Oregon Trail in this unique covered wagon made from a shoe box. The wheels are made from tagboard with small dowels serving as the axles. Punch holes in the center of the wheels and color in the spokes. To save the holes from wearing through, glue small tow washers on either side of the wheel hole. Add the wagon tongue, hitch up your mules and "Head 'em West!

ART SHOW

RODEO

best vest in the west...

Run a BEST VEST contest. Have your kids make vests out of large brown bags or wrapping paper; then decorate with crayons or markers.........

Use a chair as the horse or a carpenter's sawhorse for your roping contest. Have the "horse" set a distance suitable for your age group's capabilities. Set your own rules. Who will be the first to "rope the horse"? You might even divide your group into teams and line them up in a "rope off."

Have your kids draw pictures depicting the Early West for entry into the WILD WEST ART SHOW. For variety, make available a number of different materials, i.e. collages, pastels, crayons, paints, markers and clay for modeling.

Western Art

OVER THE BARREL

put barrels on their sides...leap over them in relay race activity

This part of the rodeo must definitely be held out of doors! Anchor the barrels by piling dirt against the sides. This will stabilize the barrels as the children leap over them. Line up two or three barrels in a row. Divide your class into teams and run relay races.

RODEO DAYS

stagecoach race

"Hitch" up two children by putting a rope under both of their arms. Another driver then picks up the two ends and drives them over the trail. The stagecoach covering the distance in the shortest period of time is declared the STAGECOACH CHAMPS.

FAST SHOOTERS

A rubber band and peanuts aimed at a target will satisfy even the worst outlaw. The rubber band is held like a slingshot. Mark a target area over which the children shoot their peanut.

PRIZES

Have each student make a tin badge out of gray tagboard. Make ribbons of different colors for different events. Winners of each event will staple their winning ribbons to their badge. Hopefully, lots of kids will win ribbons. Mix up your teams so that one team doesn't win all of the ribbons. Other prizes might include a horseshoe, a jump rope, a show ticket, etc.

set up a maze of barrels.

...for young wranglers to gallop through.....

Have a rope jumping contest as one of the rodeo fields of entry. Your wranglers must jump with both feet. How many jumps can one make in 20 seconds? That student who completes the most jumps wins!

chuck wagon

How about a real Western meal? Choose from these:

Pancakes and Sausages
Tacos and Beans
Doggies in the Saddle
Dried Beef
Bacon Bits

Stake a claim

Have each student "rope off" a given area and then list on a clipboard EVERYTHING, both living and non-living found within that area.

Invite a jeweler to come to your class to make a presentation. Ask him to bring some pieces of gold as well as samples of other precious metals. Have him relate to students information concerning the price of various precious metals as well as their different uses and what makes them valuable. You might also bring in a local rock collector to explain his hobby and to show your students his collection.

Strike it rich

ON A WORLD MAP SHOW CHILDREN WHERE GOLD CAN BE FOUND.

Find different sizes of rocks. Paint them gold and hide them for your children to find. Offer those gold foil wrapped chocolates to the winner.

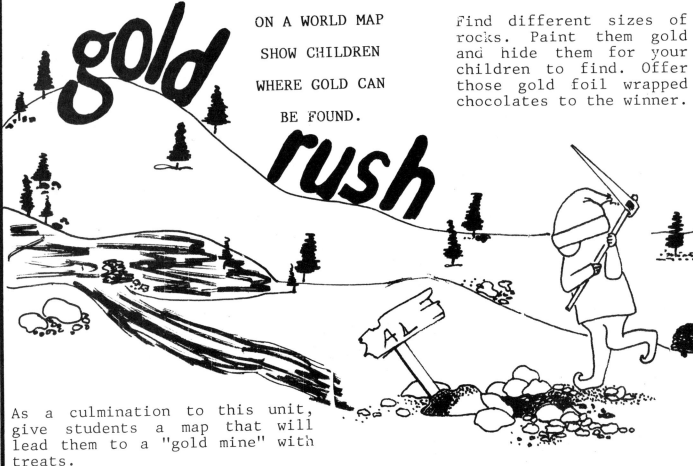

gold rush

As a culmination to this unit, give students a map that will lead them to a "gold mine" with treats.

What's the West without cactus? With an opaque projector, make this one about five feet tall. Draw it on stiff cardboard and cut both of the cacti, one from the top and one from the bottom.

Plant a cactus garden in an old cake pan. Try to get a variety of plant life.

Slide them together and spread apart. Add detail with magic markers. Hang boot-shaped task cards on the cactus.

Find out all you can about ORGAN PIPE CACTUS MONUMENT and SAGUARO NATIONAL MONUMENT.

The plural of cactus is cacti. Can you think of other similar singular-plural sets

alumnus
alumni

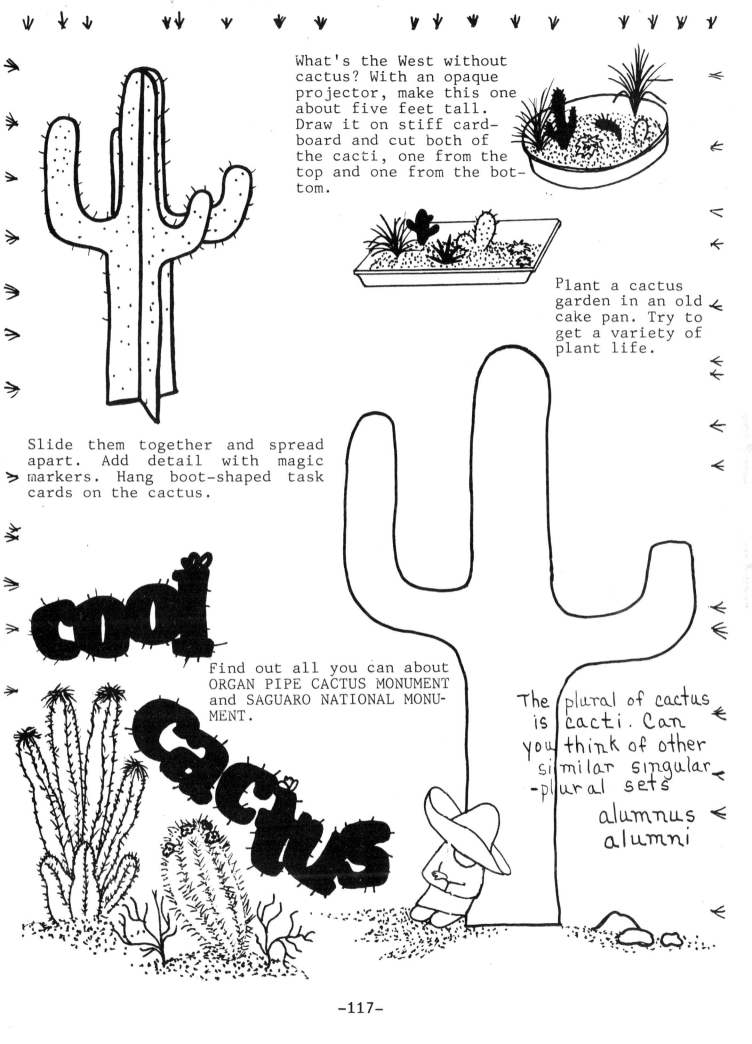

-117-

'round 'em up

'em up

head 'em up

'em up

move 'em on......

Here is your chance to write a story about the WEST. Write the copy you plan to hand in on this page.

_____

_____

_____

_____

_____

_____

_____

_____

_____

_____

_____

Purchase a class-size package of indi-
vidually-wrapped candy corn and try the
activities described below.

Corn-fetti
Mathtivity

begin with an orange triangle~

Add the white top and yellow at the bottom!

white

yellow

fold here to form a pocket!

Type the following activ-
ities on half-sheets or
write them on the board:

How many pieces did you have in your package?
Was it the same as the person who sits next to
you? Add the number you had to the class graph.
Write four complete sentences describing the
candy. Make a list of all the words you can think
of that begin with the "k" sound of the letter
c. How long a line will your candy make if the
pieces are placed end-to-end?

If you're opposed to candy, try peanuts!

Corn-fetti MIX

Cut out large candy-corn shaped pieces of paper. Write blends and digraphs on half of them and word endings on the other half. Use scrap laminating film to make a pocket inside a file folder as shown.

Add half sheets of scrap paper for students to use in keeping track of words they make. Who can make up a list of 20 new words?

Corn-fetti Shake 'n Take

Using orange railroad board, cut 36 candy corn pieces. Add details with contact paper or markers. Write words on both sides of the pieces. Students take turns spilling the can on the playing surface. Players may keep as many pieces as they can read. Allow each player three minutes to read as many words as possible. Use an egg timer to time players. At the end of each three-minute round, the winner is that player with the most correct words read.

Corn~fetti Trail

Prepare a folder game board by attaching wrapping paper to a colored file folder with spray glue. Cut out enough paper candy corn pieces to make a trail over the game board. Write one of these words on each: <u>what</u>, <u>where</u>, <u>why</u>. You will also need to make a stack of cards with phrases like "the grizzly bear" and "near the huge pool of water."

Players draw cards to determine which questions their phrases will answer. Each player then moves the appropriate number of places. Make the phrases more difficult for older children. Use phrases from basal readers for youngsters in primary grades.

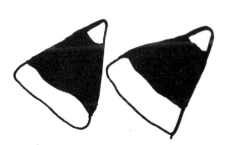

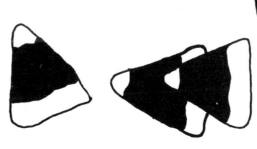

Sentenced to.....
PUNCTUATION PRACTICE

Choose any words you like to fill in the blanks below. You must, however, watch the punctuation pattern. If you have trouble, look in your reading book or the newspaper for sentences which fit the same pattern.

1 _____ _____ _____.

2 _____, _____, _____ _____
_____ _____;

3 _____! _____ _____ _____ _____
_____!

4 _____?

5 _____ _____ _____ _____?

6 _____ _____, " _____ _____ _____ _____."

7 _____! _____ _____ _____ _____?

Name_____

MONKEY-ing AROUND

Monkeys are so dearly loved for their fun-loving capers that we thought it a good idea to turn learning into "MONKEY BUSINESS." Create a jungle climate by making tall trees and hanging apes. Vines can be made by draping rope covered with twisted strips of crepe paper; then hang those monkeys from them. Keep your room filled with green palm fronds--again made from paper.

Sit under one of the palm trees for ten minutes; then write down the thoughts you had under the tree.

Have your PE teacher come in and teach your children about the safety rules necessary for using the monkey bars.

Then go do a few swings from the monkey bars, first using both hands...then one.

Have a monkey brought in from a local pet shop.

Get this poetry book from the library:

Time for Poetry
Arbuthnot, May Hill
Scott Foresman Company

Print these poems on cards for students to memorize:
   "So Many Monkeys"
   "The Monkeys and the Crocodile"
   "Monkey, Monkey, Moo"

   Make math fact ditto sheets that become more fun when called MONKEY SHINES.

Have children write short poems using all "m's."

a GRApE ApE

To make this folder game board, use a bright pink or green folder. Use large green gummed circles for the "path." To play the game a player may get on the ape trail at any point and travel in any direction. Divide the bananas equally among the players. The first player rolls the die and moves in any direction the indicated number of spaces. If he has a banana with a word that begins with that letter, he moves his marker to that spot, pronounces the word and feeds that banana to the GRAPE APE.

A player may attempt to move in either dir-ection, but if he cannot, he must wait until his next turn. The first play-er to feed all his bananas to the GRAPE APE is the winner.

Type directions for all folder games and glue to back of folder so they will be laminated along with the rest of the folder. Then everyone will know the rules.

This game can be played with this number of children. Always mark game folders in similar fashion to avoid arguments.

Tropical Treats

COCONUT TREATS: Make these during the Monkey Island stay.

Put graham crackers in a pan.
Sprinkle 1 tsp. brown sugar on each.
Put ½ tsp. butter on the sugar.
Put 1 T. coconut on top.
Place them under the broiler until the coconut is brown and the butter is melted.

Read the stories of Rudyard Kipling in The Jungle Book. You could put the stories on tape, or make dittos containing questions that relate to the various stories.

THE BANANA SPLITS

Make banana splits if your budget allows.

Shout Banana!

Cut several yellow cards in the shape of a banana. Place math facts on them and divide evenly among players. With all piles face down in front of players, each player then draws one card and turns it over. The first to shout "Banana" when two cards are turned over that are the same wins all cards that have accumulated in the center fron non-matching plays. The winner is that player who accumulates the most cards when all cards have been turned over.

GO APE OVER THESE

MARVELOUS MONKEYS:

One monkey stands in front of his group with a stack of drill cards in his hand. Two children are assigned the same number, starting with the number 3 and going as high in number as there are children in that group. You can use any numbers you wish to drill on. The leader calls out a combination (like 4 + 5 = 9).

Those two children who have the number 9 must quickly exchange places because the lead monkey is going to try to steal one of their places. To avoid confusion, you might like to have the children hold the answer number in their hands. That way you will know if the right players exchanged places.

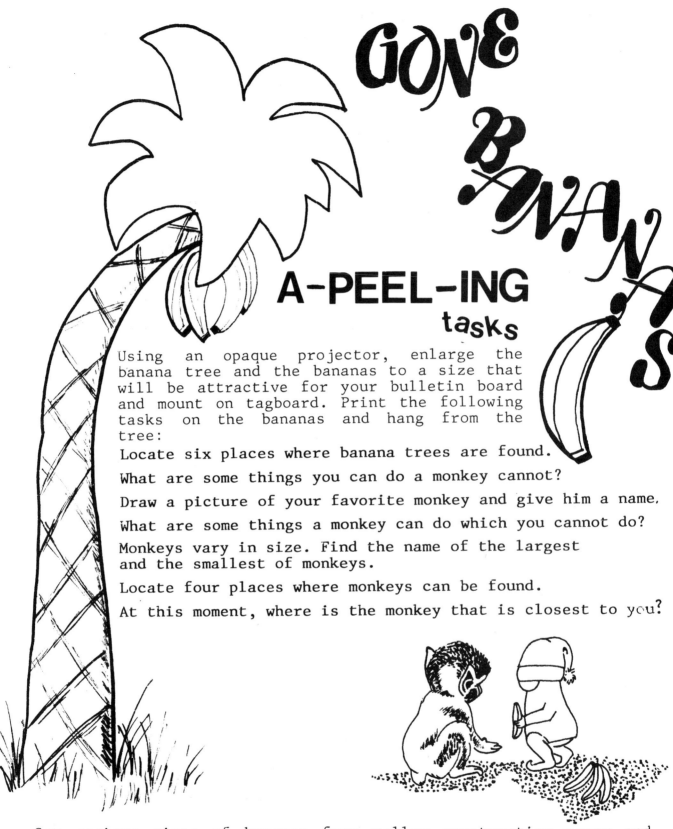

GONE BANANAS

A-PEEL-ING
tasks

Using an opaque projector, enlarge the banana tree and the bananas to a size that will be attractive for your bulletin board and mount on tagboard. Print the following tasks on the bananas and hang from the tree:

Locate six places where banana trees are found.

What are some things you can do a monkey cannot?

Draw a picture of your favorite monkey and give him a name.

What are some things a monkey can do which you cannot do?

Monkeys vary in size. Find the name of the largest and the smallest of monkeys.

Locate four places where monkeys can be found.

At this moment, where is the monkey that is closest to you?

Cut various sizes of bananas from yellow construction paper and place numbers on them. Tape them all over your room and give your children metric rulers. Use one of the monkey illustrations and make a ditto page that has bananas and numbers on it. Have your students find and measure the bananas, then put those measurements on the corresponding numbers on the ditto sheet. Place an answer key near the Monkey Island center for student convenience.

BANANA NUT BREAD

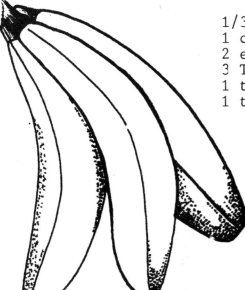

1/3 c. butter	1/2 tsp. salt
1 c. sugar	2 c. flour
2 eggs well-beaten	3 bananas or 1 c. smashed
3 T. sour milk	1 c. nuts (optional)
1 tsp. soda	
1 tsp. baking powder	

Mix together and bake in bread pan at 350 for one hour.

Use these **MONKEY TALES** as story starters...

The monkeys are coming...

I shook the monkey's hand and...

I climbed the banana tree and what did I see?

I finally met a monkey who talked and...

There was nothing to eat on the island but bananas..

Monkeys are...

The day my dad brought home a monkey...

Marvin, the window washer, was really a monkey....

And who has ever heard of purple bananas?

NEWSPAPER BANANAS

Crunch old newspapers into the shape of bananas and tape as you go. Tear strips of paper toweling in layers and paste with very thin paste. To avoid mold, allow each two or three layers to dry before adding additional layers. After it is thoroughly dry, paint yellow and glue on green roving yarn so that you will have something to use in hanging them from trees.

MONKEY SEE

MONKEY DO

Here is a sheet of writing paper. Have your students use it for the various writing assignments in this section.

JuNGLE JuMP

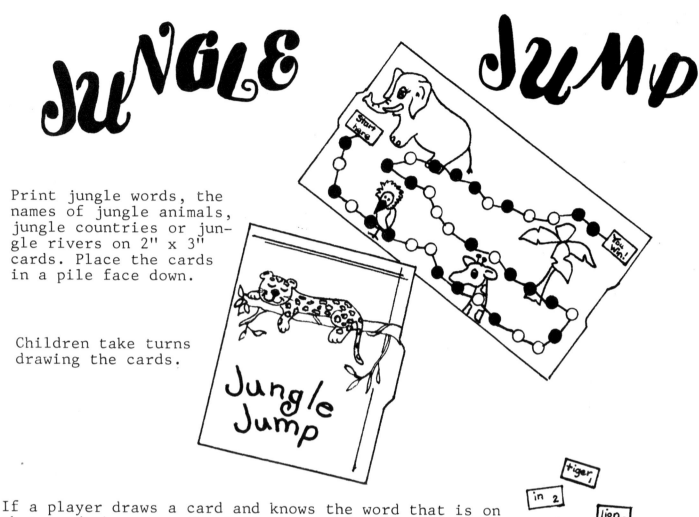

Print jungle words, the
names of jungle animals,
jungle countries or jun-
gle rivers on 2" x 3"
cards. Place the cards
in a pile face down.

Children take turns
drawing the cards.

If a player draws a card and knows the word that is on
that card, he moves the indicated number of spaces found
in the upper right hand corner of the card. If he doesn't
know the word, he passes to the next player. Decorate the
board with appropriate jungle-type paper and laminate.

MONKEY

Have your kids make monkeys from brown construction paper in the various positions you see on the pages of this unit. Hang them from vines and trees in your room and outside your door to welcome visitors to MONKEY ISLAND.

MONKEY AROUND with some addition/subtraction/multiplication/division problems. Use any of our drawings and create ditto pages with math facts to be practiced. Number them and they can become part of the banana-task card requirements.

swinging along

Label an old nail key **A BARREL OF MONKEYS**. Put stories in about monkeys. Place the number of stories to be read on banana task cards or make a separate sheet for recording the number of books you want them to read.

Make several monkey tails of various lengths out of construction paper. Provide a number of tape measures for student use in measuring the length of the tails. Which is the longest? Which is the shortest? What is the average length of the tails? Put numbers on the tails so students can check their measurements against a student answer key near MONKEY ISLAND.

BUSINESS

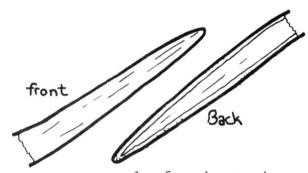

Create this "cage" effect from a 12" x 18" sheet of brown construction paper. Cut 1/2" strips from yellow paper to serve as the bars. Bow them out as you paste them on to create a three-dimensional effect.

front

Back

Here are some palm fronds to decorate your island that are made from reeds. Cut desirable lengths and glue on fringed green tissue paper. Add to a carpet roll painted green and brown to simulate the "frayed" bark of a real palm tree. Anchor these trees by pinning fishing line to your ceiling to add stability.

Make monkey masks out of brown and pink construction paper. Punch holes near the ears and let children wear them as they recite a poem about monkeys.

Who can draw the best jungle picture?

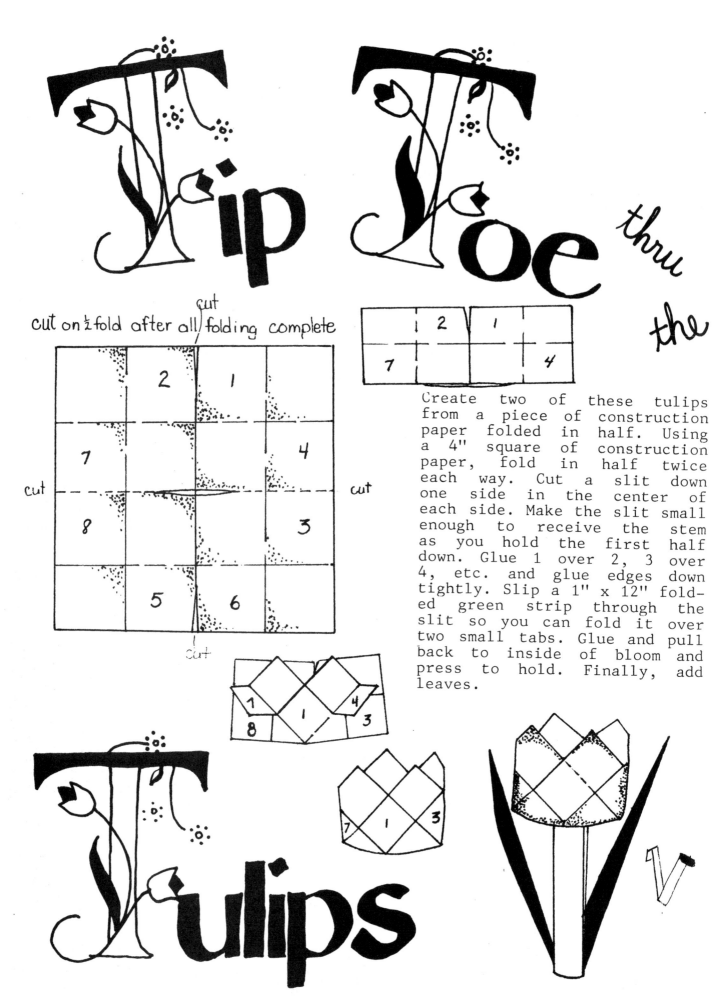

Tip Toe thru the

cut on ½ fold after all folding complete

cut

	2	1	
7			4
8			3
	5	6	

cut

cut

cut

	2	1	
7			4

Create two of these tulips from a piece of construction paper folded in half. Using a 4" square of construction paper, fold in half twice each way. Cut a slit down one side in the center of each side. Make the slit small enough to receive the stem as you hold the first half down. Glue 1 over 2, 3 over 4, etc. and glue edges down tightly. Slip a 1" x 12" folded green strip through the slit so you can fold it over two small tabs. Glue and pull back to inside of bloom and press to hold. Finally, add leaves.

Tulips

-132-

get into the *spirit* *spirit* *spirit* of the season

It's one of the kids' favorite times of year. Share it with them through these orange and black learning activities.

Begin by getting some of those real spook stories from your library.

Start each day with a Halloween poem. It's great for creative writing!

Don't forget to get your costume ready for October 31!

Find an old broom for use in a little broomstick math...

Boo-tiful Ideas for

BATWORDS are made by simply cutting bat shapes from pieces of black cardboard. Write Halloween words on white paper and paste one word to each bat. Hang them from strings over your Halloween center or in a Bat Corner. Change the tasks children are to perform with the words each day. EXAMPLES: Put them in alphabetical order; Write a question using each word; Pick five words and use them in a paragraph; Choose eight words and scramble the letters...then have a friend unscramble them; Divide a paper into nine squares and then illustrate nine of the BATWORDS.

A SLIP OF THE WAND

Enlarge the picture to the left on a piece of orange cardboard. Make the end of the broom become a pocket by gluing down only the edges. Cut narrow strips of colored paper and slip into pocket. Write a sentence or word phrase on each slip. The witch, however, has cast her spell on the illustrations so they are silly! Examples: Draw four purple pumpkins siting in an oven; The cat is vacuuming the haunted house. Use vocabulary appropriate to the level of your kids. A little humor goes a long way in motivating youngsters to read and draw. Students should copy their sentences on the bottom of the pictures. You can then hang them on an orange and black bulletin board.

Halloween Search answers

Answers to Halloween Word Search are:

> goblin
>
> ghost
>
> witch
>
> house

see page 140

Language Arts

Use the worksheet on the next page to happily mix the spirits of the season with learning. Duplicate one sheet for each child. Have them each keep a list all week of words with a double e or double o in them. Offer suckers as prizes to those who have the longest lists.

Start

The Winner!

MONSTER WORDS

Put Monster Words here!

Put used cards here!

Here's a ghoulish way to tackle those words that are especially tough for your children. Place each one of these "monsters" on a 2" x 3" card cut from orange cardboard. Students roll the die and move indicated number of spaces. They must then read one of the monster words. If they cannot, they must move back to their original place. Consider having several decks of cards adjusted to various student reading levels. Students with unlike abilities can play together if each uses his own word cards.

Make gameboard by projecting picture with overhead projector on black cardboard. Add path and details with white adhesive paper. Glue to heavier cardboard.

Monster Words

-135-

The Eeeee Ooooo contest

How many words can you think of that have EITHER two e's (which make the long sound of e) or two o's (which make the long sound of oo as in school)? You get one point for each syllable and a 10 point bonus for any word you have that no one else has. Happy word hauntin'!

Name_____

-136-

Hanging Cats and Old Bats

Using the picture as a pattern or by using a coloring book picture for a pattern, cut out one cat for each word family of rhyming words your students are working on. Give one cat to each student or to each team of students. Have them add the rhyming words to a piece of black yarn which is stapled to the cat as shown. Use "at" word family to demonstrate the concept to the class.

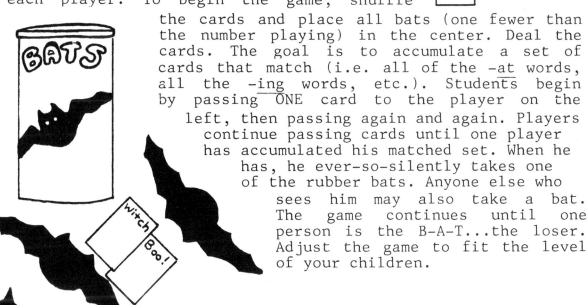

OLD BATS is a game played by a group of up to six students. To make the game, you will need a number of rubber bats, a coffee can covered with contact paper for storage and a set of cards. The cards should be prepared in sets with each set containing three related words (synonyms, adverbs, etc.). Use one set of cards for each player. To begin the game, shuffle the cards and place all bats (one fewer than the number playing) in the center. Deal the cards. The goal is to accumulate a set of cards that match (i.e. all of the -at words, all the -ing words, etc.). Students begin by passing ONE card to the player on the left, then passing again and again. Players continue passing cards until one player has accumulated his matched set. When he has, he ever-so-silently takes one of the rubber bats. Anyone else who sees him may also take a bat. The game continues until one person is the B-A-T...the loser. Adjust the game to fit the level of your children.

Witch-ful Thinking

Writing Warm-ups for Halloween

witchouse

Use black and orange paper chains to create a special corner in your room. You might call the area WITCHOUSE.

Place a tape recorder inside with the "story of the day" recorded on a cassette for the children to listen to at their leisure.

book of brews

Why not create a Class Cookbook prepared by your resident witches? This activity is well-suited for younger children. Have them write recipes for Bat Stew or Toad Popovers, etc. Add a few illustrations for flavor and place all recipes in a big black (plastic) cauldron for others to read.

mini boo!ks

Have your children create Halloween-shaped mini books. The shape could be a witch's hat or a ghost. In these mini books can be written short Halloween stories. The size makes the project of writing less threatening to small children who often have difficulty with such assignments. You might even have the children write stories without words.

ghostories

Let your kids try their hand at writing ghost stories on ghost-shapes made out of tissue paper using fine line markers. To help them in organization, try working on the beginning of the story one day, the middle the next day and the ending on a third day. Hang final drafts on a bulletin board display after students have shared their spook stories with each other.

Have students write HORROR-scopes for each other!

The Pumpkin Path

Begin by cutting a pumpkin-shaped game board from a sheet of orange cardboard. Add stem and face with markers. Cut out pictures of words with beginning or ending sounds your kids need to practice and glue them to board. Students roll die and move indicated number of spaces if they can pronounce proper sound. If they cannot pronounce sound properly, play passes to next player.

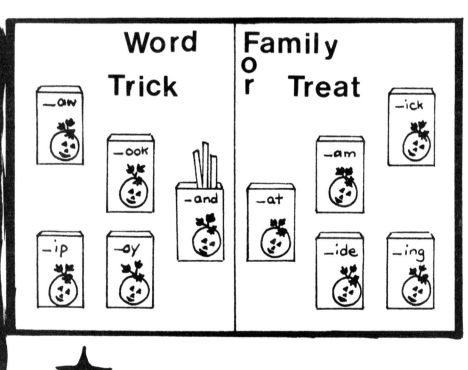

This simple activity can be completed by one or two students to reinforce word patterns as shown. Begin with a piece of cardboard which you have painted orange or covered with contact paper.

Glue small bags to board and laminate. Write word patterns on each bag. Kids can check on each other. You can also substitute file folders for bags if you like. Have students choose five of the words and write sentences about them.

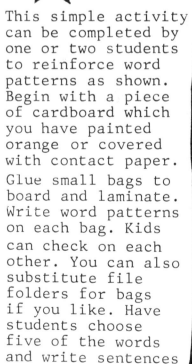

Find the hidden Halloween word in each of the shapes below by crossing out every letter you find printed more than once. Then rearrange those that are left to form a word we associate with the Halloween season.

a n j m d t a e
r f r g i z c s
b q u i u b z q
k v c p v w e i
y f w x h y k l
o m x j d p n a

w k g e c d h g
a d b j l k l j
m p s f u e q r
r s o q u v x a
z y t v o i x b
y p f n z m e n

Spellbound Words

f g n f c k m
l q e s v m j a
p w j a r u f d
y n w x k y o d
e s x b q h r t
n t p u c v f i

u m b n j d e f
l b t o q r p c
t l p w f n g r
w c g d v h a k
k v i y q i x k
c s y m j n x a

The answers to this word search are found on page 134.

Let's put some live action into Halloween with a real CREATURE FEATURE. First we must find a critter. Look in the corner of your garage or under a rock ...or any other place a spider might be hanging out. Once you've found a volunteer, guide him gently into a jar and truck him off to school.

To create your SPIDERARIUM you will need a large glass jar with a cover containing holes smaller than the spider. Place a layer of soil in the bottom and add a few twigs and leaves. Place a piece of wet sponge to assure proper moisture. You may also need to add a few bugs occasionally for food. Duplicate observation sheets for all students with questions and facts of interest to your students.

Scour your school library for books, filmstrips, tapes and pictures of spiders to add to your SPIDERAMA. This might also be a good time to begin the classic Charlotte's Web. It's a favorite among children with a chapter a day providing a meaningful fill-in for those extra moments.

Place sentence strips on the table for student use. As they find out facts about spiders, they write them on the strips. Place them in web.

SPIDERS

several creepy ideas for Halloween science

Single egg carton sections make good bodies for spiders. After the children have had a chance to observe the class spider, have them make their own spiders. Use egg carton sections for bodies and pipe cleaners for legs. Mount them on a black paper web...or hang them from the ceiling...or add them to a spider bulletin board.

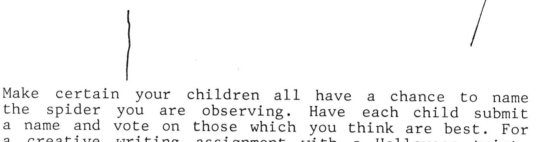

Make certain your children all have a chance to name the spider you are observing. Have each child submit a name and vote on those which you think are best. For a creative writing assignment with a Halloween twist, use spiders as the subjects of cinquain poetry.

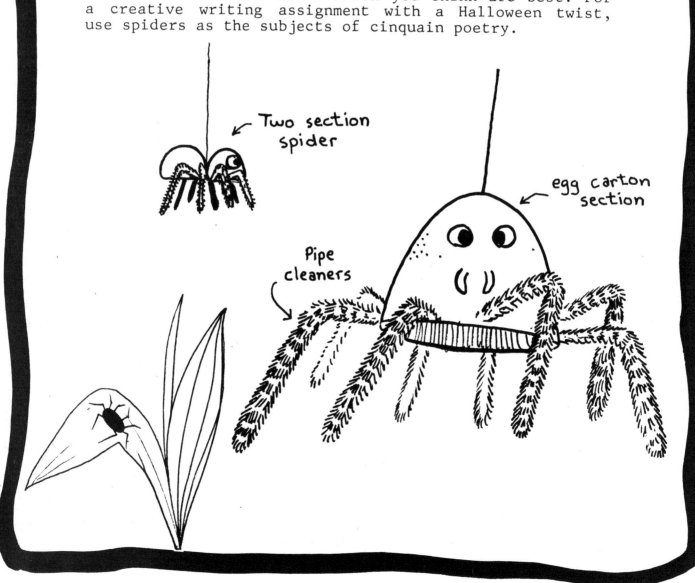

Two section spider

egg carton section

Pipe cleaners

Spider Watch

1. Look closely at your spider. How many legs does it have?_____

2. Make a mark with your crayon that is EXACTLY the color of the spider. [ ] What other colors is it?

_____

3. Does it have eyes? _____ feet?_____
antennae? _____

4. what four words describe it best?

_____ _____ _____ _____

5. Finish this sentence:
This spider is big as a _____,
a _____, or a _____

It's the Clean Desk Witch!

I peeked in yours and it's spook-tacularly clean!

I'm bewitched
by clean desks!

A Halloween Hooray
for you!

Insert an orange sucker through the above hole.
. . . . . distribute appropriately . . . .

SPOOK-TACULAR ★ WORK!!

Congratulations, _____!

Your work in _____

was great! Keep it up!

from _____

ORANGE TRICKS 'N TREATS

Here's a fun treat for your Halloween party...or for the day when everyone passes the spelling test. Prepare a can of frozen orange juice. Orange Kool—Aid will also provide a cool orange treat. Cut the tops off sticks of black licorice for children to use as straws.

Prepare finger Jello or regular orange Jello in small plastic containers. Allow them to harden and let students add jack-o-lantern faces with an aerosol can of frosting.

How about trying some sand-WITCHES by cutting pieces of toast or bread into witch shapes with a cookie cutter? Or perhaps you could make triangular witch hats.

Using your favorite recipe for play dough, make a large batch of red and an equal amount of yellow. Let your kids mix the two together to make orange play dough for use in making pumpkins. Mini pumpkins can then be dried and worn on chains.

A bag of real oranges may be the best treat of all! Decorate with markers and eat or float orange slices with frosted faces in punch!

Packages and

Place a class treat in a shoe box and cover with endless layers of tissue paper, crepe paper, newspaper, etc. Select one of the games below and you're ready for some fun!

Using a marker, write a math problem on each layer. Have your kids sit in a circle. The first player unwraps the first layer and hands the box to the person next to him. The player can unwrap the next layer if he can answer the math problem. Play continues until students get to the SUPER treat. The treat, of course, should be shared by all.

Rather than the math problem, this time write directions about who shall open the next layer. For example: "Give to the person with the longest hair," "Give to the person with a birthday in October," "Give to the person who is wearing gold tennis shoes," etc.

You can also use this activity as a relay, but you will need one package for each team. Add directions on each layer as you wrap. For example: "Hop on one foot," "Make a noise like a bat," etc. Students line up in relay fashion. After one student completes his task, he passes package to next team member who will then unwrap next layer and do the assigned task.

1 package 3 ways

Party Games

WANDERING WARLOCK: Children sit in a circle on chairs. One child is WARLOCK and stands in the center without a chair. WARLOCK names a category (children with a short vowel in their name or kids with brown socks). Those who fit into that category quickly exchange chairs with others. The last child standing becomes WARLOCK for the next round.

SKELETON SCATTER: Find three Halloween pictures (student drawings or pictures out of magazines) and cut them into puzzle pieces. Hide the various pieces around the room, holding back one key piece from each puzzle. Divide children into three teams. Give each team their key puzzle piece. Their task is to find all of the pieces and assemble the puzzle correctly.

THE WITCH'S SOCK: Fill a man's black sock with a variety of items including keys, a comb, a pen, a small apple, an eraser, a flashbulb, a glove, etc. Each student will need a piece of paper and a pencil. Have students pass the sock around the circle. Each student is allowed to feel the sock. Players then write down as many items as they can remember feeling. Empty the sock and that student with the greatest number of correct items is the winner.

GHOST BAG SCRAMBLE: Make white bags out of old sheets. Glue scrambled Halloween words onto small blocks of wood and place inside the bags. Make one bag and one set of words for each group of children. At a given signal, dump the words out on the floor and each group tries to unscramble its words. The first team to complete the unscrambling of its words is the winner.

Invite a cat — a real, live black-is-best cat to visit today. What adjectives describe it? How does it look? sound, feel? Is it — maybe-magic?

Disguises of a Different Dimension

Discount store costumes are okay, but you can generate a little creativity and reduce your expenses by trying one of the ideas that follow:

Plan for some very simple costumes this year by setting up a disguise table in one corner of your room. Add a mirror plus a number of jars of facial creams. Kids can even add hats to their disguises, but costumes from the neck up are the rule of the day.

Paper bags or pillow cases can also be used as costumes with the only investment being a little creativity. Have each student work on his costume during his free time. Hang old sheets to create an environment of privacy for times when kids are working on their costumes.

An alternative to paper bags and pillow cases is a grocery carton. These costumes can either be made at home or at school. Have a parade through the hall to allow your kids to share their colorful accomplishments with others. As a lasting memento of the occasion, line them all up for a picture.

Colored paper and cardboard can add a lot to Halloween happiness without adding much to cost or preparation. Begin by making task cards using the pattern found on this page. Write tasks that relate to things you have in your Halloween center, or perhaps you may want to assign some tasks to do with real pumpkins.

PAPER PUMPKINS

Ideas for task cards could include: Make a skeleton out of black paper and white straws; Find ten words that tell about Halloween; Make a pumpkin puzzle; Draw a scary picture; Weigh a pumpkin.

PAPER PUMPKINS

witch's handbook

Make Witch's Handbooks by putting a piece of writing paper on top of a sheet of orange construction paper and then folding it in half from the top down. Cut pumpkin shape leaving stem as only remaining folded part. Students write things inside.

Place a sheet of writing paper on top of a sheet of orange construction paper. Fold in half and trim to a pumpkin shape. Now glue writing paper to construction paper. Kids then write "Halloween is..." on the outside of their pumpkin and finish the sentence and then illustrate inside.

pumpkin house

pumpkin wheel

Have students cut three pumpkins at one time from orange construction paper. Fold each in half and glue adjacent sides till pumpkin stands by itself. Students can use one section to gather pumpkin nouns, another for pumpkin adjectives, etc.

PAPER PUMPKINS

front

slit here

add book pocket on the back

pumpkin slots

Cut pumpkin shapes from a sheet of orange construction paper. Add a slit in the middle the entire length of the top edge of a book pocket. Glue a book pocket to the back side of the pumpkin to enable slips to be placed through the slot. Students can add a slip every time they read a book or complete a perfect paper. You might also consider putting assignments on half-sheets and placing them in the slot. Put each child's name on the front.

Cut a pumpkin pocket from orange felt and stitch around the lower edge as shown. Place the "Treat of the Day" in that pocket. Perhaps you might use a ghostly crossword puzzle, a riddle or a special Halloween story.

pumpkin pocket

PAPER PUMPKINS

Pumpkin Pop Outs

Make these simple, self-checking pop-out pumpkins by beginning with a stack of cardboard pumpkins which you have made by using the one on this page as a guide. Make a stack of ghosts as shown and cut pumpkins in half. Join both halves with a brass fastener. Add math problems or other information which children need to practice. Store them in a plastic pumpkin.

89, 90, ___ 92

89, 90, 91 92

For this activity you will need a plastic pumpkin, two flashlight batteries, wire, a flashlight bulb and cardboard for making the playing cards. It should also be noted that this activity is somewhat time consuming.

Pumpkin Lights!

lead a   lead b

flashlight bulb

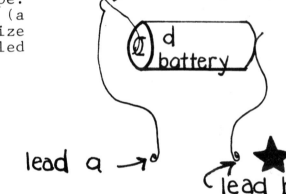

To prepare the pumpkin first wire the two size D batteries as shown. Strip the ends of insulation and attach tightly with friction tape. Make certain that lead wires (a and b) are long enough to minimize the change of their being pulled out.

front

Try These
- 6 × 9   • 25
- 3 × 8   • 63
- 5 × 5   • 24
- 8 × 6   • 16
- 9 × 7   • 54
- 4 × 4   • 48

lead a →

lead b

Place problems all on left side of card and answers on right side. Be certain to mix them up. Then insert a brass fastener next to each question and answer. Connect each question and answer on the back side of the card with a wire that has been stripped on both ends. Cover back of card to conceal wires and backs of fasteners. Players should place lead a on a problem and lead b on the answer. If the answer is correct, the pumpkin will light up. An incorrect match will result in the pumpkin remaining dark.

back

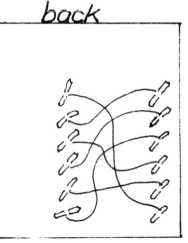

WB

This is the perfect time of year to stimulate young imaginations. A few sheets of orange and black paper plus a touch of white paint can bring out the "witch" in the best of them. Have them tear ghostly shapes from tissue paper and mount them on black paper. They can add details with scraps of paper or collage materials. Try holding your own "Design-a-Witch" contest. Assign a special place on your bulletin board for this Ghastly Gallery of the Gruesome.

Witch Crafts

haunted milk cartons

Milk cartons make the ideal beginning for haunted houses. Have children begin by covering their milk cartons with strips of paper on the lower half and square pieces folded in half that cover the roof. Kids then add details with foil, white paper and whatever else they find in the scrap box. A smaller apartment-size version can be fashioned out of a quart size carton.

BLACK AND WHITEWASH

Give each student a piece of black paper and a black crayon. Instruct students to draw Halloween pictures using only the black crayon. Motivate with a spooky record in the background. When pictures are finished, apply a watered-down coat of white tempera for some frightful fun!

BATPUPPETS

To make bat puppet, fold a 12" x 18" sheet of paper in thirds. Then fold in half. Finally, fold the top edge down and the bottom edge back. Cut wings from a second sheet and glue to front fold. Add details Do bats have eyes? What does it mean to be "blind as a bat"?

PUMPKINSTICKS

Your kids will also enjoy making large cellophane pumpkin masks. Make a circular frame out of cardboard or construction paper and glue on orange cellophane. Students then add jack-o-lantern details with scrap construction paper and staple to a dowel and you have an inexpensive Halloween mask.

BROOMSTICK MATH

Here's the perfect use for that scraggly old broom you've been wanting to throw away! Create a crepe paper cobweb in the corner of the room and station your broom directly under the web. Then prepare math problem cards in the shape of spiders to hang from the web over the broom. You should also assign a Witch of the Week to check the work of those doing the problems. Have your "witch" dress in black to add to the atmosphere.

Here are some suggestions for task cards:

How long is the handle? Measure in centimeters?

List three things longer than the handle.

Find something in the room that is exactly the same length

Pull out a bristle and use it to measure. How many bristles is it to the water fountain?

Measure six things in your home with the bristle and report your findings to the class.

Are all bristles the same size?

NOVEMBER

S	M	T	W	TH	F	S
Sing a happy song today!	Eat lunch with a new friend today.	Whisper something nice to someone.	Make someone giggle!	who has the longest leg in your room? Measure.	How many words can you find in Thanksgiving?	Help someone at home today. Try hard!
	Trace around your hand. Write 5 things you're thankful for.	"Goody Day." Have a piece of corn candy!	Measure to find out who has the longest hair.	Wear something brown!	PLEASE!! Pick up litter today!	
	Surprise Day! Don't open until 2:30 p.m. ?!?	Find pictures of turkeys.	Let's cook cranberries! Yum!	Tell 1 thing about Pilgrims.		
			Write a Thank You note to someone.	Make a feather and wear it.		Have a nice weekend.

Happy Thanksgiving!

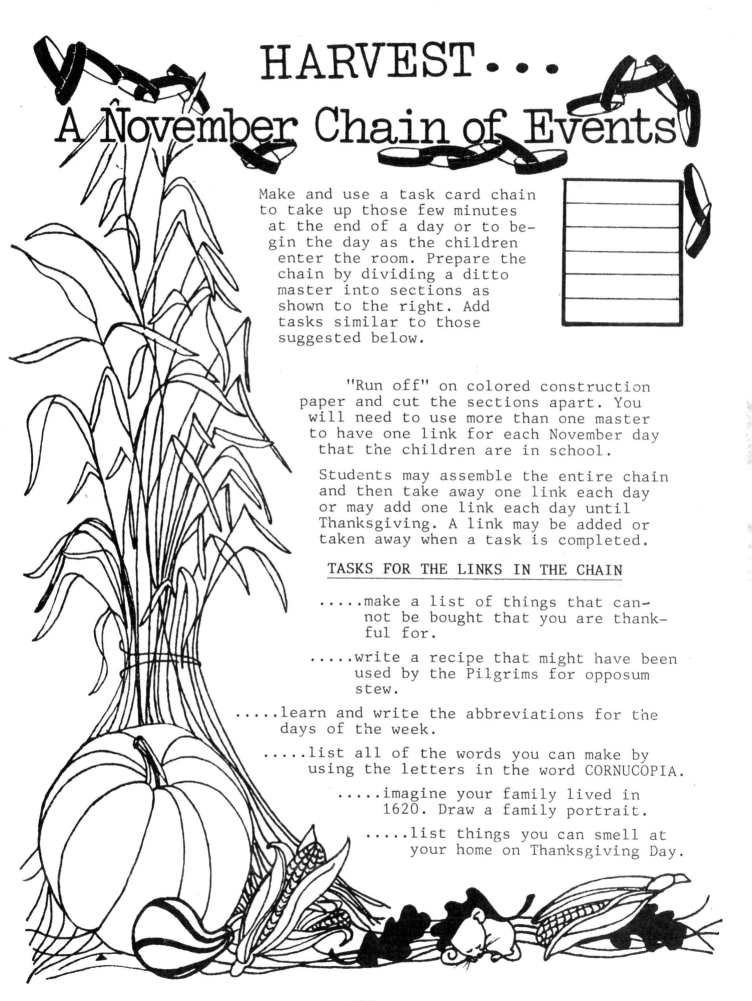

HARVEST...
A November Chain of Events

Make and use a task card chain to take up those few minutes at the end of a day or to begin the day as the children enter the room. Prepare the chain by dividing a ditto master into sections as shown to the right. Add tasks similar to those suggested below.

"Run off" on colored construction paper and cut the sections apart. You will need to use more than one master to have one link for each November day that the children are in school.

Students may assemble the entire chain and then take away one link each day or may add one link each day until Thanksgiving. A link may be added or taken away when a task is completed.

TASKS FOR THE LINKS IN THE CHAIN

.....make a list of things that cannot be bought that you are thankful for.

.....write a recipe that might have been used by the Pilgrims for opposum stew.

.....learn and write the abbreviations for the days of the week.

.....list all of the words you can make by using the letters in the word CORNUCOPIA.

.....imagine your family lived in 1620. Draw a family portrait.

.....list things you can smell at your home on Thanksgiving Day.

Have a....
Happy Harvest

Harvest has been a happy time in many cultures
through many generations. We hope the ideas that
follow will help you harvest some good ideas for
a bountiful learning experience.

TO BEGIN: Lay a foundation for the Thanksgiving
holiday by helping children understand the vocabulary which
might be used. Duplicate copies of the front cover of a
Thanksgiving Dictionary (sample below). Add blank pages
and a blank back cover. At the bottom of each page have
students write one vocabulary word. Older students can use reference books to define and illustrate the words. Younger children
will need to learn through teacher directed class discussions.
Words to use might include: pilgrim, bountiful, harvest, England,
Mayflower, Mayflower Compact, Samoset, Massasoit, Squanto.

Thanksgiving Dictionary

name_____

HARVEST...

TURKEY PULL is a game which can be used to reinforce sight words. Using the opaque projector, enlarge the gameboard as shown. The white areas are separate pieces (see pattern below). Add slits at the base of the white areas. Write the words to be practiced on the separate pieces. Insert the feather pieces from the back of the gameboard. The pieces should move in and out easily.

Turkey
Pull

Students roll a die and move from feather to feather from the bottom row to the top row. Students pull out the feather they land on and read the word. They may stay on the word if they can read it. First to reach the end wins.

language arts ideas

Put a circle around the things you see in the picture.
five horses   two dogs
two men fishing
a girl feeding geese
smoke coming out of the chimney
green leaves

Colored file fold-
ers add an inter-
esting dimension
to game-making.

Use a magazine picture
on one half of the in-
side of the folder.
On the other half,
add directions for
students to follow.
Laminate. Students
follow directions
using crayons
or grease
pencils.

Begin with a pizza board.
Add the Thanksgiving details
as shown. Put one half of
a compound word on the board
and the other half on a
pinch clothespin. Students
match the clips to the board
and make a list of the compound words they were able
to form. You might also ask
students to pick 5 words
and use them in a sentence.

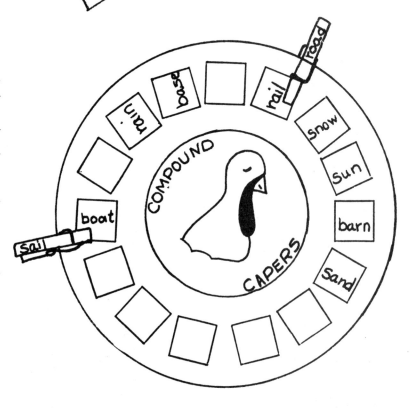

COMPOUND CAPERS

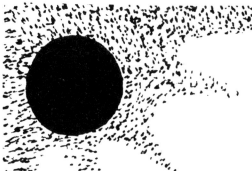

...and more
Magazine Mix

Magazines have helped take the tedium out of seatwork. Add these three ideas to your collection of magazine magic.

1. Glue seasonal pictures to one side of colored file folders. On the opposite side write questions that have multiple choice answers. Laminate the folders and have students use grease pencils or crayons to circle the correct answers.

Circle the right answer:
1. How many pumpkins do you see?
   11   13   15
2. How many people in the picture?
   one zero six
3. How many bushels of fruit do you see? 9

cool   clear   straw   bent   dusty   rough   boo   orange

2. Use magazine pictures to work on grammar. Have students write appropriate adjectives all over a picture from a group you have selected. One point is awarded for each appropriate adjective the student thinks of. The same can be done with verbs and nouns.

3. Prepare gifts for parents using magazines and ice cream containers. Each student is given a clean but blank container. For each book a child reads he can glue on one magazine picture of his choice. By Christmas all students will have a gift that's meaningful to both parent and student. Of course, the increased reading is a great side benefit.

language arts ideas

Fit-A-Feather

Begin with a colored file folder. Add the turkey as shown. In each feather add a slit for a paper clip. Make separate corresponding feathers with opposites, synonyms, homonyms, identical words written in cursive. Students match loose feathers with words written on the folder and slip them in the clip. Store loose feathers in an envelope taped to the back of the folder.

Orange and Yellow Relay

This game is a relay and a relay can add a little zip to almost any reading or math group lesson. A relay is an excellent "Friday" activity. Divide your group into two or more teams. Each team will get a stack of orange word cards which should be given to the person in the front of the relay line. A group of yellow cards is given to the person at the end of each relay line. The object of the game is to get the orange cards to the back of the line and the yellow cards to the front of the line. This is done by passing the cards overhead from player to player. Each player must read each word out loud. The first team to achieve the switch wins the game. This game may be somewhat confusing to very young children. It is excellent for older children who need many reinforcements to achieve mastery of sight words.

or "Draw Three"

Enlarge and cut two copies of the bushel basket. Staple the two pieces together to form a pocket. Put the letters from a large seasonal word like NOVEMBER or THANKSGIVING inside the pocket. Students singly or in teams of 2 or 3 draw 3 letters and list as many words as possible that have those three letters in them. Reproduce the worksheet below for the students' work.

DRAW THREE
The 3 letters I drew
_____ _____
are in......

name_____

Dig out some of those books in your school library filled with seasonal poetry! Use some of the activities listed below to help youngsters get a feel for the abbreviated writing. Enough exposure to good poetry will give them confidence to write their own.

HARVEST • • • •

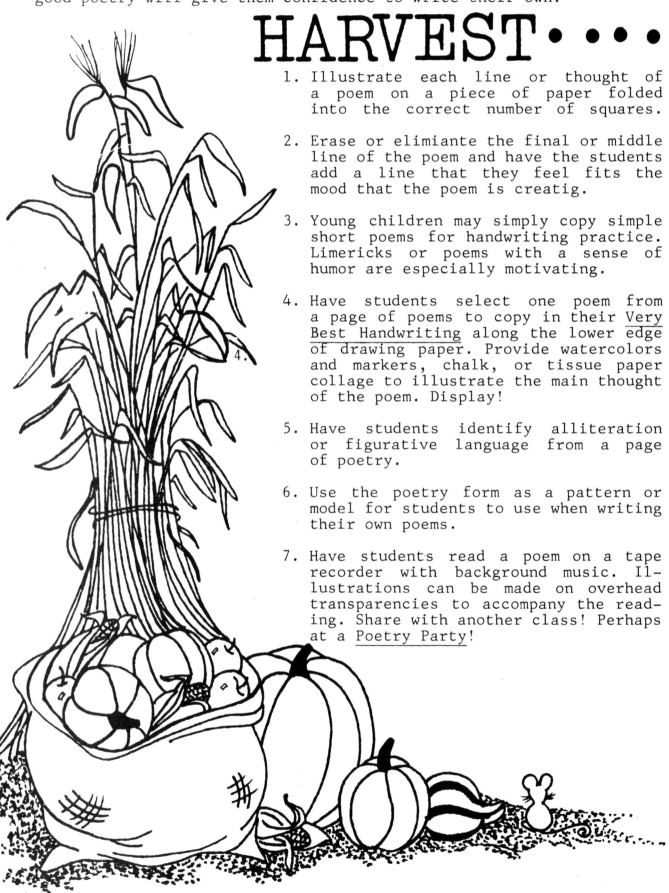

1. Illustrate each line or thought of a poem on a piece of paper folded into the correct number of squares.

2. Erase or elimiante the final or middle line of the poem and have the students add a line that they feel fits the mood that the poem is creatig.

3. Young children may simply copy simple short poems for handwriting practice. Limericks or poems with a sense of humor are especially motivating.

4. Have students select one poem from a page of poems to copy in their <u>Very Best Handwriting</u> along the lower edge of drawing paper. Provide watercolors and markers, chalk, or tissue paper collage to illustrate the main thought of the poem. Display!

5. Have students identify alliteration or figurative language from a page of poetry.

6. Use the poetry form as a pattern or model for students to use when writing their own poems.

7. Have students read a poem on a tape recorder with background music. Illustrations can be made on overhead transparencies to accompany the reading. Share with another class! Perhaps at a <u>Poetry Party</u>!

15 ideas for poetry punch!

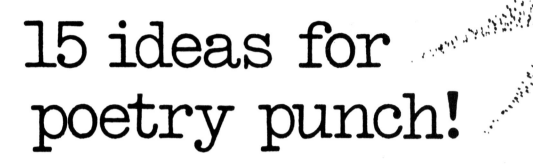

8. Make a class MAXI book of favorite poems.

9. Have the students memorize one poem.

10. Use the simple poems or finger plays as dialogue for paper bag puppets. Trees and wind can become puppets too!!!

11. Have students locate all 1, 2, or 3 syllable words in a poem.

12. Do something different with the same poem every day for a week.

13. Do the same activity every day for a week with different poems!

14. Have students write the poem on the top half of their writing paper and write four facts about the author on the bottom.

15. Have students write synonyms or antonyms for words you've underlined in one or more poems.

HARVEST.....
a game for ANY skill

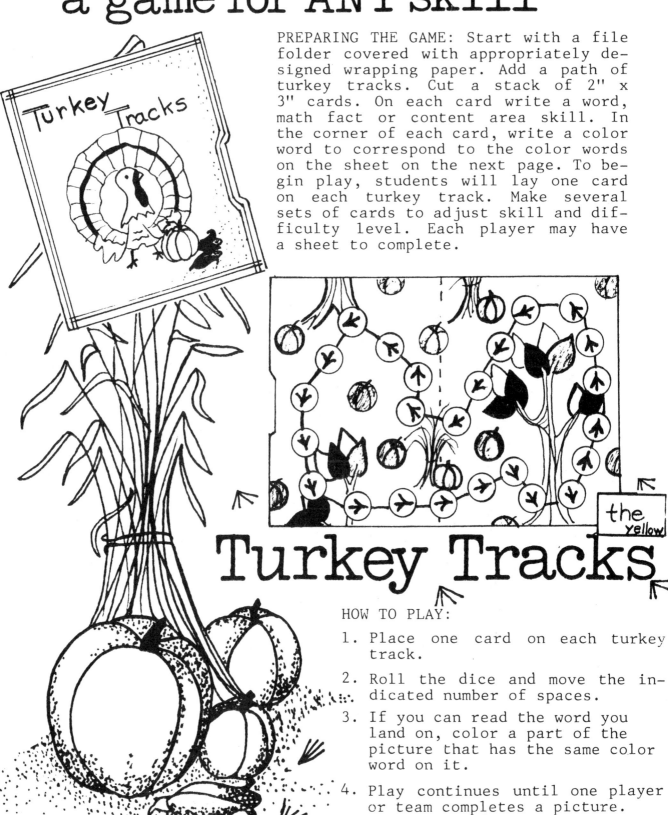

PREPARING THE GAME: Start with a file folder covered with appropriately designed wrapping paper. Add a path of turkey tracks. Cut a stack of 2" x 3" cards. On each card write a word, math fact or content area skill. In the corner of each card, write a color word to correspond to the color words on the sheet on the next page. To begin play, students will lay one card on each turkey track. Make several sets of cards to adjust skill and difficulty level. Each player may have a sheet to complete.

Turkey Tracks

HOW TO PLAY:

1. Place one card on each turkey track.

2. Roll the dice and move the indicated number of spaces.

3. If you can read the word you land on, color a part of the picture that has the same color word on it.

4. Play continues until one player or team completes a picture.

Turkey Tracks

yellow
red
red
orange
orange
yellow
yellow
yellow
red
orange
brown
green
red
red
orange
red
orange
yellow
red
orange yellow
orange
brown
green
red
red
green
green
brown
brown
brown
yellow
green
brown
yellow
orange
yellow
brown
yellow
red
yellow
yellow
orange
orange red
orange
brown
brown
red
yellow
orange
brown
orange
brown

name_____

HARVEST ·······

Have the students glue cylinders to a square of dark paper as shown. A small strip of paper curled over at one end makes the neck and head. Feet and details may be added with scraps of paper or fabric. One feather may be added for each book read or each neat paper.

Turn the cylinder the other direction and this turkey will stand without being glued down. These may be made small or large to use as Thanksgiving centerpieces. Use very bright colored paper or wallpaper for the tail feathers.

a handful of art ideas

Paper plates, either white or seasonally colored, make good beginnings for turkeys to be made by young children. Plates should be painted if white ones are used before adding the details. Add either paper feathers as shown above or real feathers (available at craft stores) as shown below. Details should be added by students without teacher directions to enhance the creativity.

Have the students cut a pear or gourd shaped piece of paper and glue it to a bright piece of 9" x 12" construction paper. Students add loops for feathers and crayon or scrap paper details.

and more....

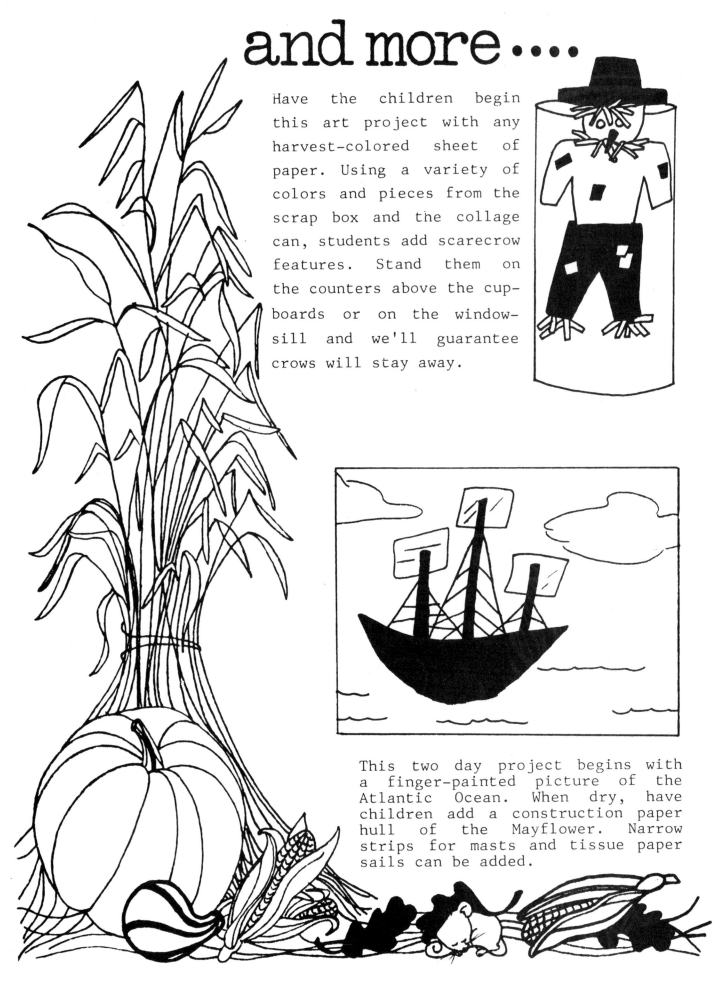

Have the children begin this art project with any harvest-colored sheet of paper. Using a variety of colors and pieces from the scrap box and the collage can, students add scarecrow features. Stand them on the counters above the cupboards or on the window-sill and we'll guarantee crows will stay away.

This two day project begins with a finger-painted picture of the Atlantic Ocean. When dry, have children add a construction paper hull of the Mayflower. Narrow strips for masts and tissue paper sails can be added.

SAVE TOM'S LIFE! DISGUISE HIM...

AS A JIVE TURKEY! OR....
A Sitting Duck, Stool Pigeon, Jailbird, Hot Canary,
Clay Pigeon, N.B.C. Peacock.....

WANTED

DEAD OR ALIVE

TOM TURKEY

FOR THANKSGIVING DINNER

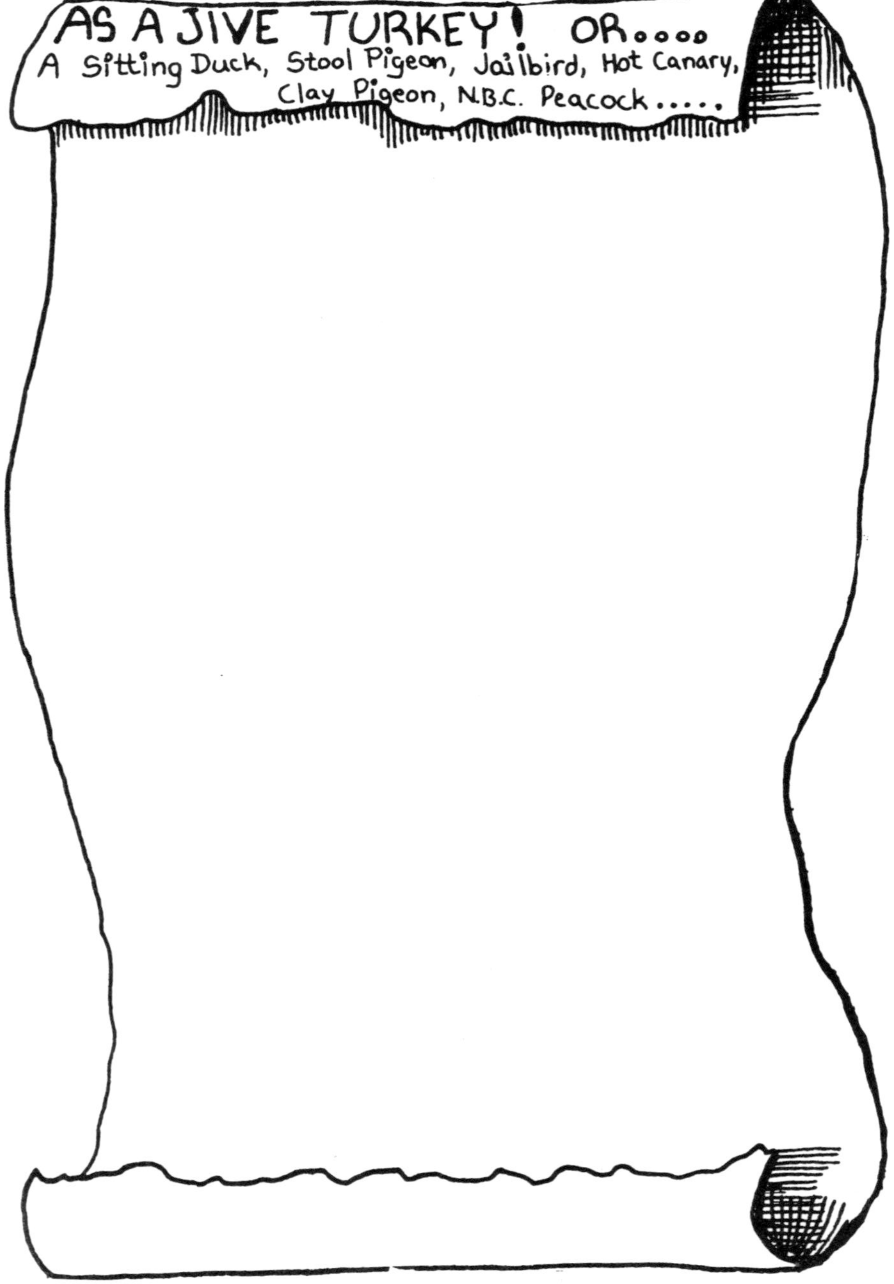

DANDY

GANDERS

<u>SO</u> <u>REALISTIC</u>.......you'll think the

flock is comin' right into your

<u>CLASSROOM</u> ! ! !

The body is made from white construction paper (12" x 18") folded in half
lengthwise to a 6" by 18" size. Then
cut this to 6" by 14". Cut the body
into a torpedo shape. Glue the body
around the edges, leaving the
neck area open. Now, stuff
slightly with crushed pieces
of newspaper or with facial
tissue. Tuck the neck into the
correct end and glue shut. The
neck should be of black paper about 3" x 6". Taper to a proper shape.
Each wing should be of brown paper about 5" x 12". Staple to the body
from underneath. Feathers can be made from tissue paper and glued to
the body. Hang in groups from the ceiling. Add eyes if desired.

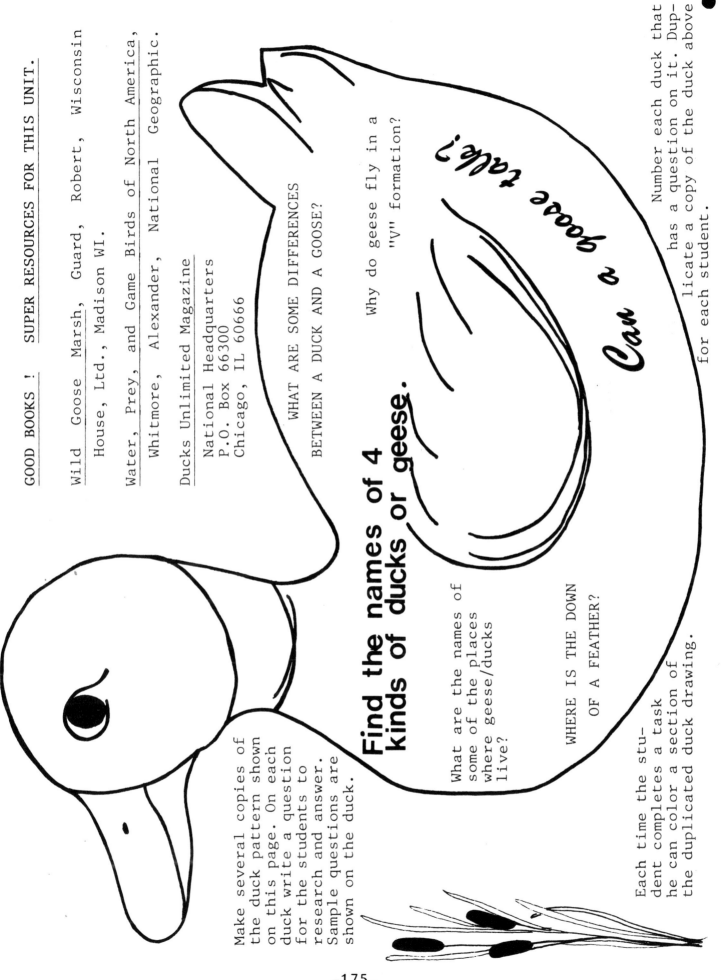

GOOD BOOKS ! SUPER RESOURCES FOR THIS UNIT.

Wild Goose Marsh, Guard, Robert, Wisconsin
    House, Ltd., Madison WI.

Water, Prey, and Game Birds of North America,
    Whitmore, Alexander, National Geographic.

Ducks Unlimited Magazine
    National Headquarters
    P.O. Box 66300
    Chicago, IL 60666

WHAT ARE SOME DIFFERENCES
BETWEEN A DUCK AND A GOOSE?

Why do geese fly in a
"V" formation?

Can a goose talk?

Find the names of 4
kinds of ducks or geese.

What are the names of
some of the places
where geese/ducks
live?

WHERE IS THE DOWN
    OF A FEATHER?

Make several copies of
the duck pattern shown
on this page. On each
duck write a question
for the students to
research and answer.
Sample questions are
shown on the duck.

Number each duck that
has a question on it. Duplicate a copy of the duck above
    for each student.

Each time the stu-
dent completes a task
he can color a section of
the duplicated duck drawing.

A

SUPER

GOOD MOVIE!

FLY GEESE FLY

A-V Productions Inc.
2000 Eggert Road
Amherst, NY 14226

A
Dan Gibson
Production

MORE for the TASK CARD DUCK...
featured on the previous page.

What other animals does man hunt?

How does a duck stay afloat on water?

What can feathers be used for?

*** *** *** *** *** *** *** *** ***

Somewhere in your area there should be a gracious person who would bring a goose, duck, pheasant or turkey to your classroom. The children could learn much from observing and asking questions.

Bring in a wildlife manager.

Have him demonstrate duck and goose calls that are used by hunters. Let him tell what management of wildlife means. Perhaps he could bring a film or an animal to your classroom.

Play the old game DUCK DUCK GOOSE!!!

MAKE

Use long narrow pieces of blue paper for background. On the paper make cattail pictures. The brown part of the cattail is made of two pieces that have been slightly stuffed. Add long slender stems and thin graceful leaves. Hang these pictures along both sides of the door or hang them side-by-side to create a marsh.

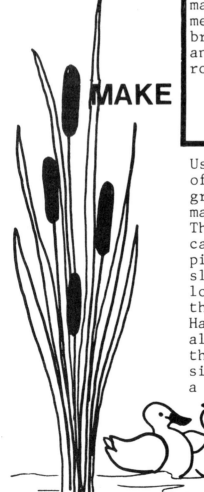

Section off a part of a bulletin board. Cut pictures from sport magazines to place around the area you have sectioned off. Let the children sign their parent's name and what they will hunt for. Discuss hunting as a sport and how years ago it was a necessity. Discuss good sportsmanship. From newspapers and magazines cut articles pertaining to the topic. Add them to the bulletin board.

WILD stories

The Lost Goose -- The Ugly Gosling
The Shy Moose -- Big Foot Appears
The Empty Forest -- and Forest Fun
are a few possible starters.

The Pilgrims came
across the sea
To find new land in which
to be.
Indians were here to
ease their stay.
Together they made
Thanksgiving Day!

We offer a combination study of Pilgrims and Indians. Please remember that when teaching about Indians that it should be done with great respect for the rich heritage they contributed to the development of this nation. Perhaps the greatest asset to a successful unit would be the contributions members of the race could relate to you and your students.

Make silhouettes of Pilgrims and Indians from black construction paper. Vary the sizes and tape to classroom windows.

Make two hats from black tagboard. They should be 7" x 9" tall. Staple a white bakery bag between the two hats. They will now stand up on a table. Place task cards in them or allow children to place notes stating what they are thankful for in them. On the day before Thanksgiving vacation have the children draw out the notes and share them with the class.

Thanksgiving is a good time to teach the children how to set a table properly. Bring a real set of dishes, cutlery and napkins. Children can take turns sitting at the table and practicing good manners.

Set a Thanksgiving table!

Have children draw around one hand. Print the word Thanksgiving in the palm....then write things they are thankful for on the fingers.

A GOOD SEATWORK ACTIVITY

On a 12" x 18" sheet of drawing paper have children cut out and paste pictures of plates and silverware, etc., from magazines. All items should be pasted in the proper place. Pictures of food could also be cut out and pasted.

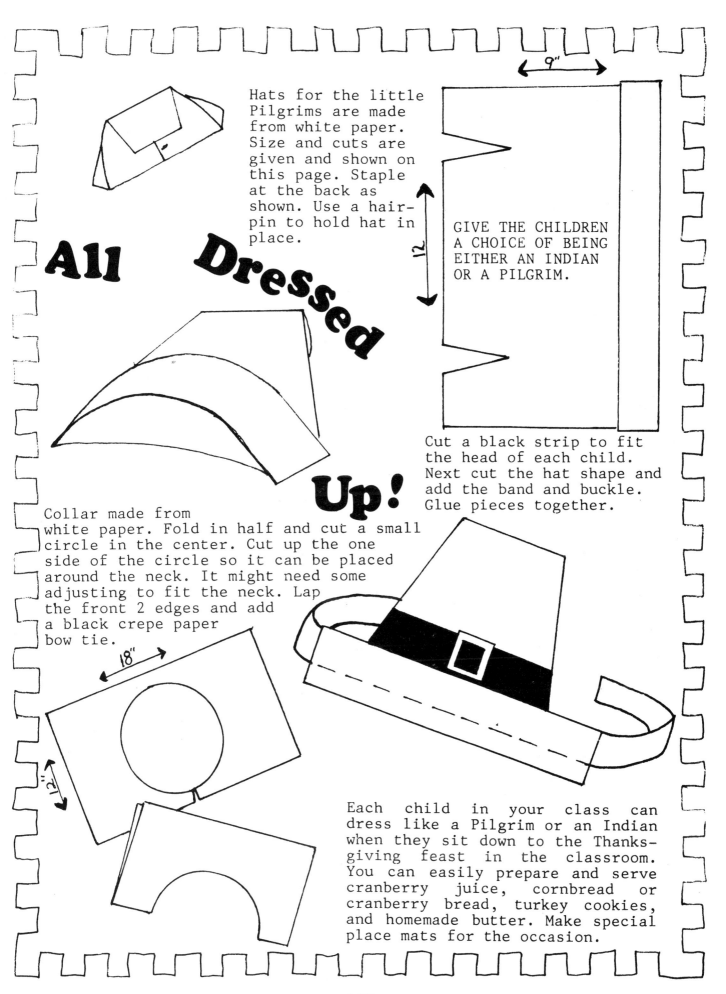

Hats for the little Pilgrims are made from white paper. Size and cuts are given and shown on this page. Staple at the back as shown. Use a hairpin to hold hat in place.

All Dressed

Up!

GIVE THE CHILDREN A CHOICE OF BEING EITHER AN INDIAN OR A PILGRIM.

9"

12

Cut a black strip to fit the head of each child. Next cut the hat shape and add the band and buckle. Glue pieces together.

Collar made from white paper. Fold in half and cut a small circle in the center. Cut up the one side of the circle so it can be placed around the neck. It might need some adjusting to fit the neck. Lap the front 2 edges and add a black crepe paper bow tie.

18"

12"

Each child in your class can dress like a Pilgrim or an Indian when they sit down to the Thanksgiving feast in the classroom. You can easily prepare and serve cranberry juice, cornbread or cranberry bread, turkey cookies, and homemade butter. Make special place mats for the occasion.

Thanksgiving Concentration

From black paper cut hats about 9" high. Staple them together as shown. Add white bands and gold buckles. Print a simple version of the Thanksgiving story on pieces of white paper and glue them to the hat sections in the proper sequence. You now have a story in the round. Set it on a child's desk and let him READ.

Glue pretty Thanksgiving paper on the inside of a colored file folder. Glue a pocket on the back of the file folder for the 16 index cards that are shown. Choose 8 Thanksgiving words. Each word should be printed on two of the cards. All cards are placed on the folder face down. Two children play the game. One turns over 2 cards. If the words are the same and the child can say the word he can select two more. If the words do not match the child turns them back over and it is the second child's turn. Who can get the most cards?

Hats Off to Learning !

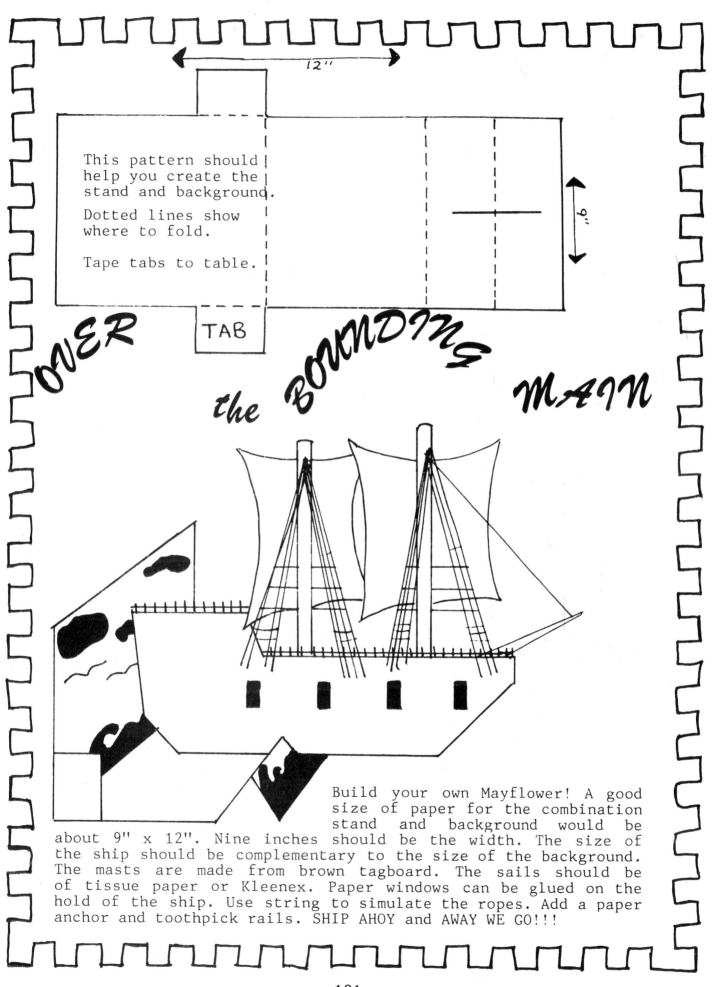

12"

9"

This pattern should help you create the stand and background.

Dotted lines show where to fold.

Tape tabs to table.

TAB

OVER the BOUNDING MAIN

Build your own Mayflower! A good size of paper for the combination stand and background would be about 9" x 12". Nine inches should be the width. The size of the ship should be complementary to the size of the background. The masts are made from brown tagboard. The sails should be of tissue paper or Kleenex. Paper windows can be glued on the hold of the ship. Use string to simulate the ropes. Add a paper anchor and toothpick rails. SHIP AHOY and AWAY WE GO!!!

Use the information on the Mayflower Math Sheet to help you find the answers to these questions. You may have to look some words up in the dictionary or ask your teacher what they are.

Mayflower Math

1. How long did the trip from England to the United States take?

2. How much longer was the Mayflower at the main hull than she was at the keel?

3. How many years ago did the Pilgrims land?

4. How much longer at the main hull was the Mayflower than at the beam?

5. Was the Mayflower longer at the keel than she was wide at the beam?

6. How many grown-ups were on the Mayflower?

7. How many of the grown-ups were NOT soldiers?

8. Which was the longest, the ship at the keel, the ship at the main hull, or the ship at the beam?

name _____

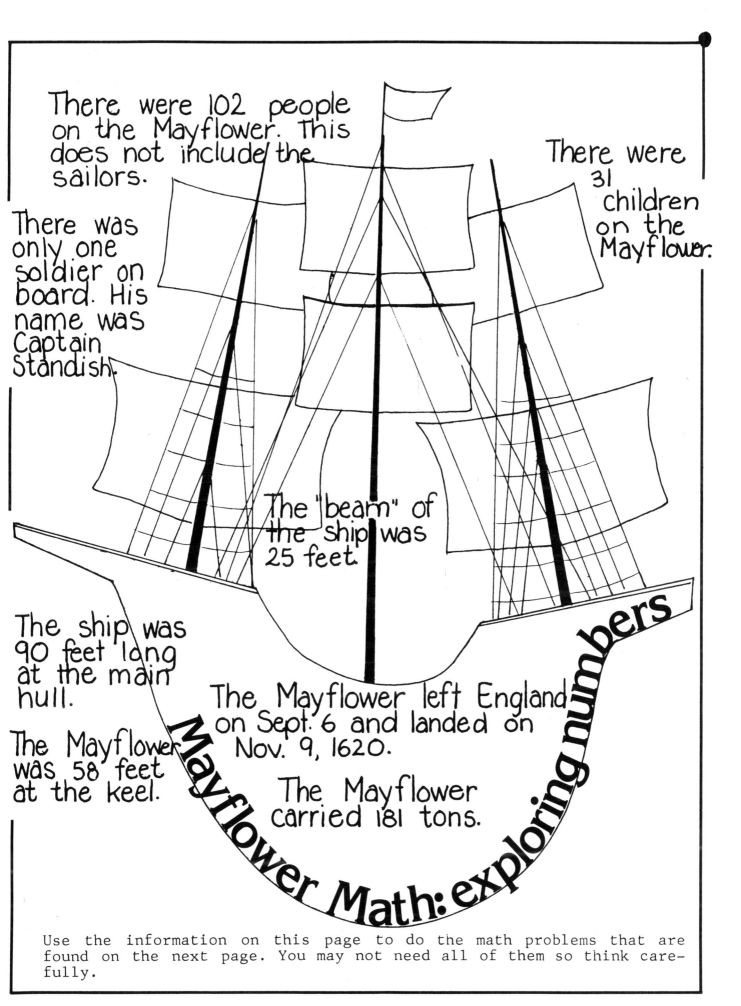

There were 102 people on the Mayflower. This does not include the sailors.

There was only one soldier on board. His name was Captain Standish.

There were 31 children on the Mayflower.

The "beam" of the ship was 25 feet.

The ship was 90 feet long at the main hull.

The Mayflower was 58 feet at the keel.

The Mayflower left England on Sept. 6 and landed on Nov. 9, 1620.

The Mayflower carried 181 tons.

Mayflower Math: exploring numbers

Use the information on this page to do the math problems that are found on the next page. You may not need all of them so think carefully.

I for each child!

The words that are printed on the pull strips can be different for each child. Base the words on the child's ability.

Use sight vocabulary words or words to learn to spell.

Instead of saying the word that is printed on the strip the child says a rhyming word.

corn
deer
pilgrim

pie

turkey
feast
Mayflower
Indian

make hat of black paper. cut slits. 1¾" x 12" white strip. write words on it.

To make the hat cover a coffee can and a pizza wheel with black contact paper. Add a band of grey paper and a gold buckle. Fill the hat with strips cut from tagboard. On each strip write a sentence for the children to copy for writing practice. Laminate the strips for durability.

Gobble! Gobble! It's turkey time.

Five turkeys sitting on a fence.

The turkey is a very funny bird.

Off we go to grandmother's house.

Will you pull the wishbone with me?

Run, Tom Turkey, run, run, run.

I just love to eat pumpkin pie.

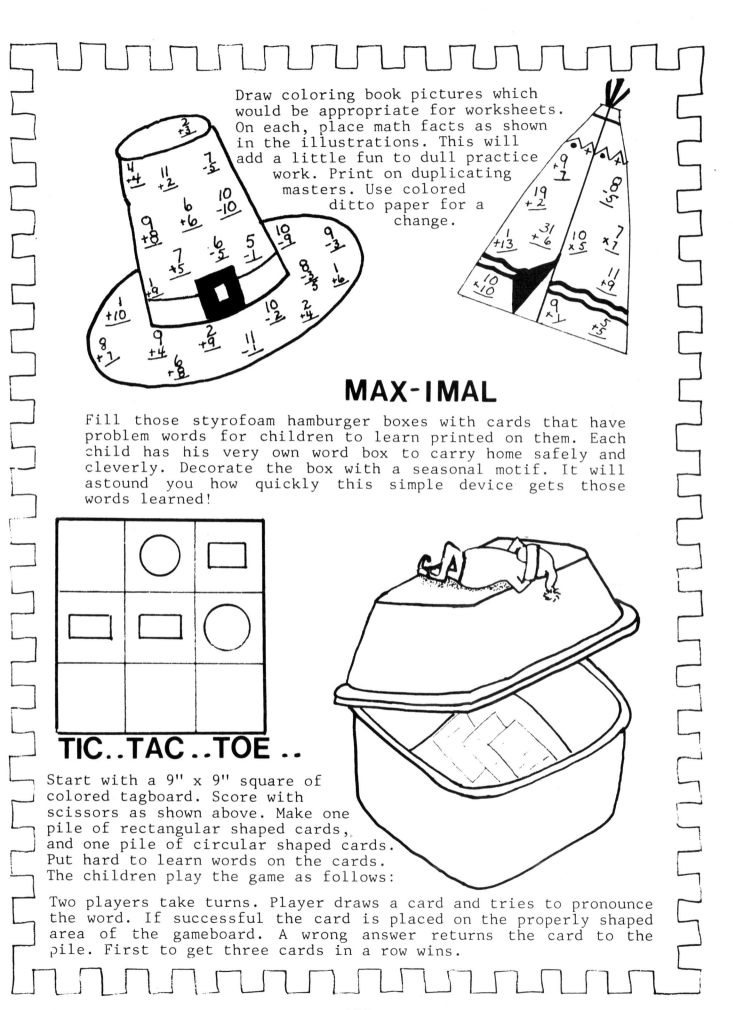

Draw coloring book pictures which would be appropriate for worksheets. On each, place math facts as shown in the illustrations. This will add a little fun to dull practice work. Print on duplicating masters. Use colored ditto paper for a change.

MAX-IMAL

Fill those styrofoam hamburger boxes with cards that have problem words for children to learn printed on them. Each child has his very own word box to carry home safely and cleverly. Decorate the box with a seasonal motif. It will astound you how quickly this simple device gets those words learned!

TIC..TAC..TOE ..

Start with a 9" x 9" square of colored tagboard. Score with scissors as shown above. Make one pile of rectangular shaped cards, and one pile of circular shaped cards. Put hard to learn words on the cards. The children play the game as follows:

Two players take turns. Player draws a card and tries to pronounce the word. If successful the card is placed on the properly shaped area of the gameboard. A wrong answer returns the card to the pile. First to get three cards in a row wins.

Make small moccasin shaped cards (about 4" x 6") from tagboard. This game is played just like Drop the Handkerchief. The child walks around the outside of the circle carrying the pack of moccasins instead of a handerchief.

Have a POW-WOW to make learning fun. Here are some games to help you.

The child drops one card behind a child and runs. The child must pick up the card and run and try to catch the first child. If he catches the child and can read what is on the card, he can be the next dropper. Math facts could be on the cards.

Make "tracks"....

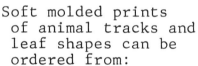

Soft molded prints of animal tracks and leaf shapes can be ordered from:

NASCO
Nature Study Aids
Ft. Atkinson, WI 53538

The children love to handle these shapes and they can be used to make prints because they are easy to wash.

Paint tempera tracks or cut tracks from paper. Place tracks on the floor and when the children arrive they follow the tracks to a SURPRISE !!!

If you do this more than once, change the footprints to those of another animal. The children can identify which animal made the tracks.

The surprise can be a new book, a game or a treat.

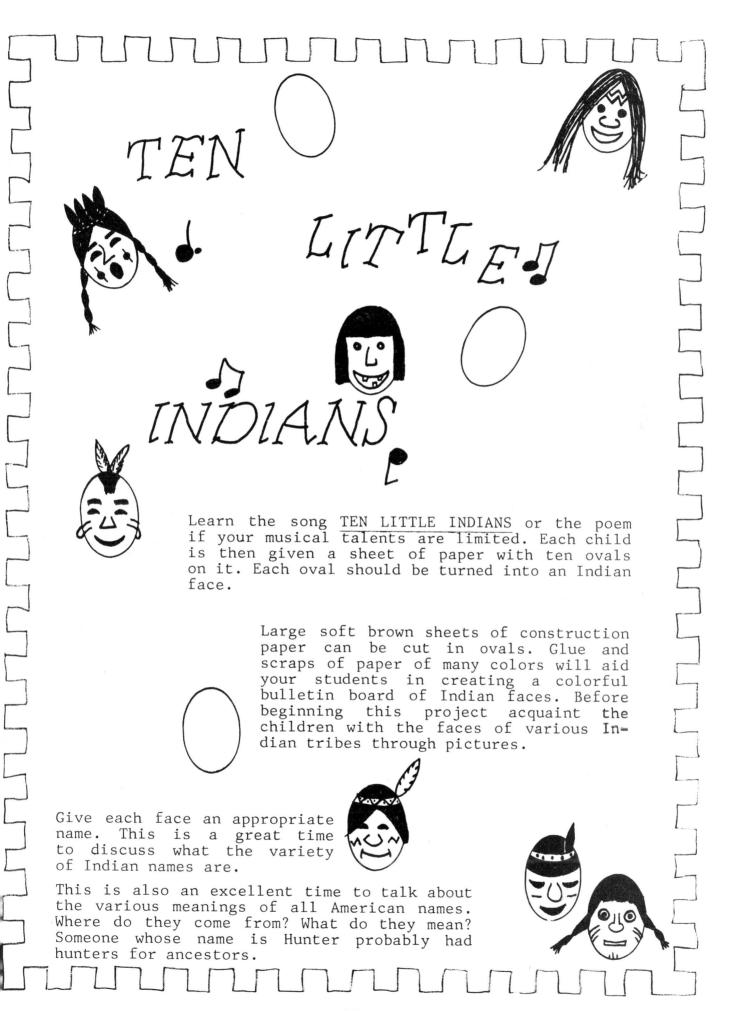

TEN LITTLE INDIANS

Learn the song TEN LITTLE INDIANS or the poem if your musical talents are limited. Each child is then given a sheet of paper with ten ovals on it. Each oval should be turned into an Indian face.

Large soft brown sheets of construction paper can be cut in ovals. Glue and scraps of paper of many colors will aid your students in creating a colorful bulletin board of Indian faces. Before beginning this project acquaint the children with the faces of various Indian tribes through pictures.

Give each face an appropriate name. This is a great time to discuss what the variety of Indian names are.

This is also an excellent time to talk about the various meanings of all American names. Where do they come from? What do they mean? Someone whose name is Hunter probably had hunters for ancestors.

Little Red Cloud peeked into the cave... 'Cause Yellow eyes and a roaring growl came out the cave. Oh, he was so very, very brave. Yellow raised his hair... grizzly big, brown, bear...!

the HAPPY TRAIL

Give children circle or triangle shaped pieces of paper. Stories or poems can be written on the paper. The stories/poems should be written round and round in a circle or triangle fashion.

Council Fire

Outside on the playground build a campfire. Gather your "tribe" around the council fire to do some planning or to have discussions. This is also a good location for a storytelling session. For a campfire in the classroom, place sticks and twigs on a small brown rug. Store in a cardboard box.

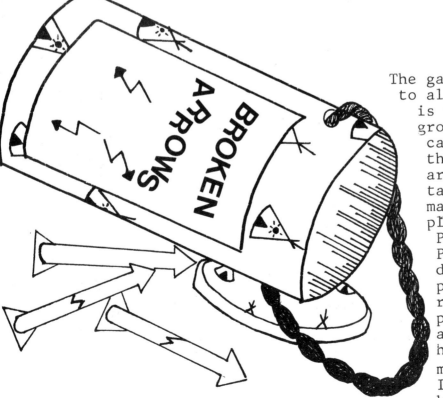

BROKEN ARROWS

The game can be adapted to all seasons. The game is used in reading groups and the winner can take it home for the evening. Make the arrows from brown tagboard. Words or math facts can be placed on the arrows. Place arrows in a Pringles can that is decorated. Player picks an arrow and reads the answer printed on the arrow. If correct he picks again. He may stop any time. If he draws a broken arrow he loses.

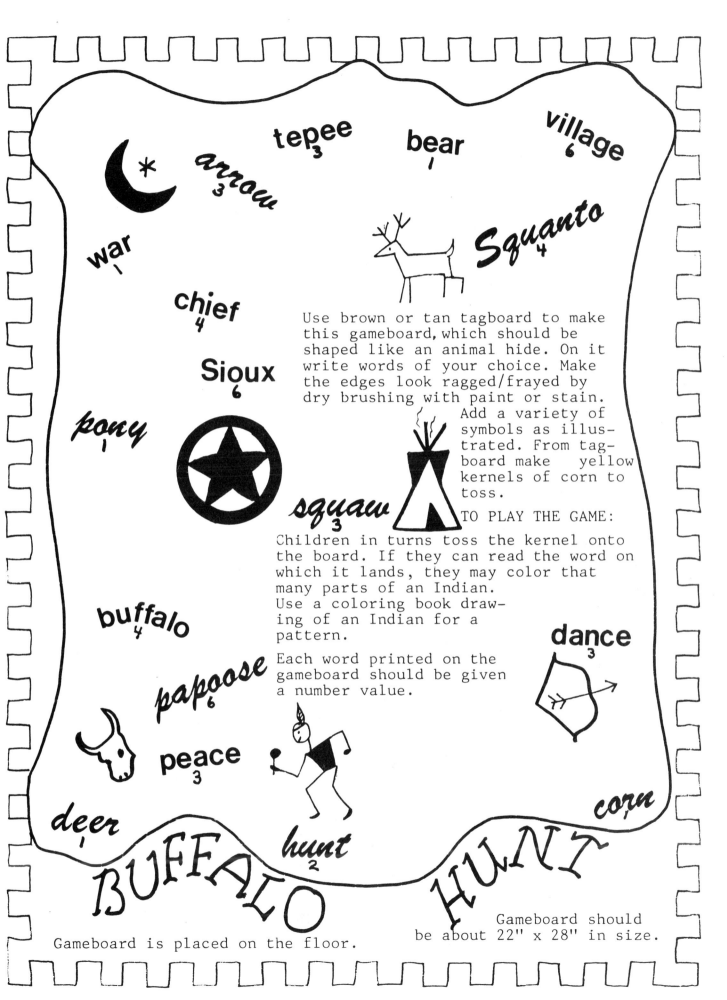

tepee
₃

bear
₁

village
₆

arrow
₃

war
₁

Squanto
₄

chief
₄

Sioux
₆

pony
₁

squaw
₃

Use brown or tan tagboard to make this gameboard, which should be shaped like an animal hide. On it write words of your choice. Make the edges look ragged/frayed by dry brushing with paint or stain.

Add a variety of symbols as illustrated. From tagboard make yellow kernels of corn to toss.

TO PLAY THE GAME:
Children in turns toss the kernel onto the board. If they can read the word on which it lands, they may color that many parts of an Indian. Use a coloring book drawing of an Indian for a pattern.

Each word printed on the gameboard should be given a number value.

buffalo
₄

dance
₃

papoose
₆

peace
₃

deer
₁

hunt
₂

corn

BUFFALO HUNT

Gameboard is placed on the floor.

Gameboard should be about 22" x 28" in size.

HIT this WORK....

Roll 4 or 5 different activity sheets together. Hold them together with a napkin ring or a section of a cardboard tube. Paint this bright orange. Glue on the tomahawk with the words "HIT THIS WORK" printed on it. When a child uses one of the sheets that was rolled he replaces it with one of the same.

To save time make several duplicated copies of each sheet you choose to include. Each week you may wish to completely change the worksheets. At the end of a specified time each child could be responsible for completing a certain number of the sheets.

BINGO!!

totem pole	chief	tribe	gobble
cabin	turkey	Mayflower	pie
gun	corn	tepee	Pilgrim
eat	arrow	goose	feast

Enlarge this matrix onto a ditto master. Run off...give each of the children a sheet and let them print in words you have written on the chalkboard. All children do not have to print words in the same squares. Play like BINGO. It's a super way to teach vocabulary. The leader gives the definition. The winner gets to be the next caller.

From tan tagboard make two of the tepees shown above. Staple a brown bag between them. Put cards with all sorts of Indian names and terms on them. Let the children practice saying the names: Cochise, Apache, Cheyenne, Chippewa, Sioux, Mohawk, Hopi, etc.

Refer to The American Indian, a deluxe Golden Book, Oliver LaFarge, Golden Press. You'll find good pictures and lots of information.

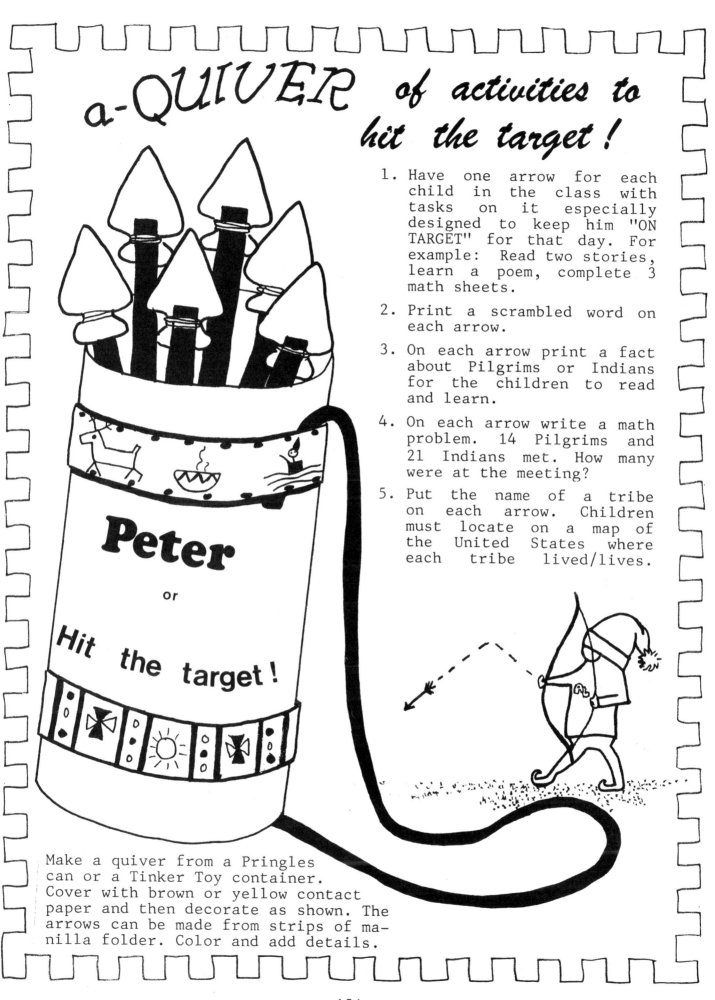

a-QUIVER of activities to hit the target!

1. Have one arrow for each child in the class with tasks on it especially designed to keep him "ON TARGET" for that day. For example: Read two stories, learn a poem, complete 3 math sheets.

2. Print a scrambled word on each arrow.

3. On each arrow print a fact about Pilgrims or Indians for the children to read and learn.

4. On each arrow write a math problem. 14 Pilgrims and 21 Indians met. How many were at the meeting?

5. Put the name of a tribe on each arrow. Children must locate on a map of the United States where each tribe lived/lives.

Peter

or

Hit the target!

Make a quiver from a Pringles can or a Tinker Toy container. Cover with brown or yellow contact paper and then decorate as shown. The arrows can be made from strips of manilla folder. Color and add details.

SMOKE SIGNALS

SEND A MESSAGE TO GERONIMO !

Give yourself an Indian name. How did you acquire it? Bravery, peace, season, big kill, wisdom?

Draw a picture of an Indian hunting for food for his tribe.

D- code
THESE WORDS !

skoem   rife

    nurb

loaffub   edre

    brite

*

Write
a message to send as a smoke signal:

to warn a war party.

that you sighted a herd of buffalo.

that a wagon train is near.

that you see some hunters.

a storm is coming.

Find some other
ways of signaling

semaphores *** Morse code

blinkers from the Navy

flags *** hand signals

**   drums

VOCABULARY WORDS

smoke	fire	burn
buffalo	deer	help
signal		

* buffalo   deer   help

signal

**

Make an Indian drum. Make a code for it and send some messages to a friend.

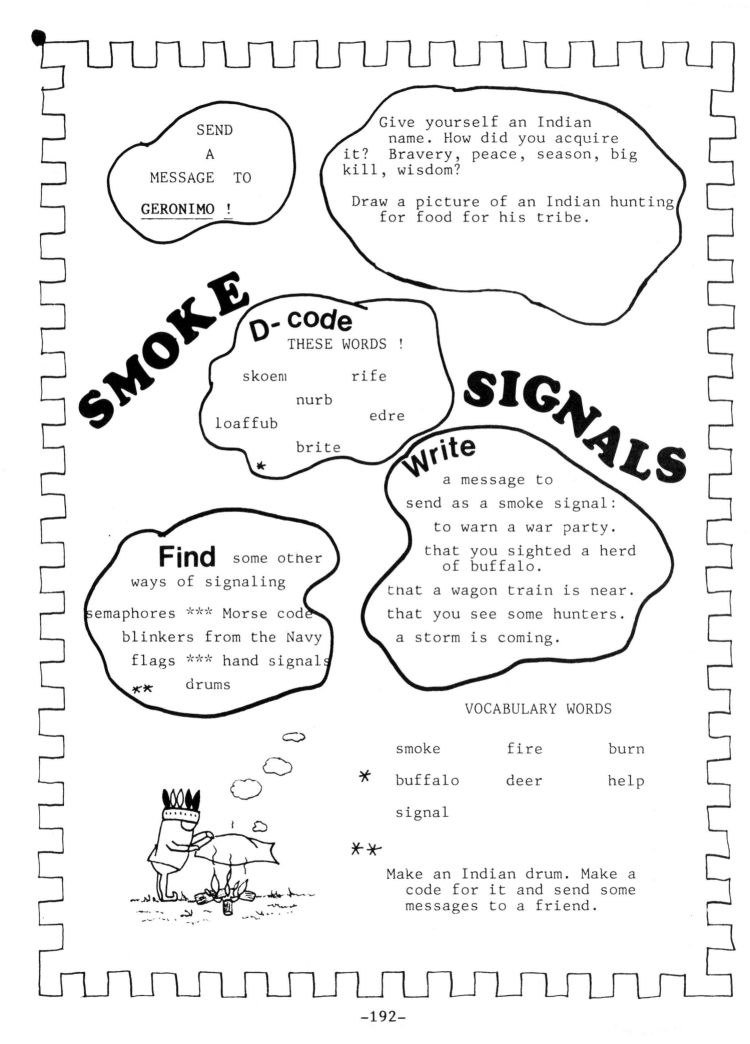

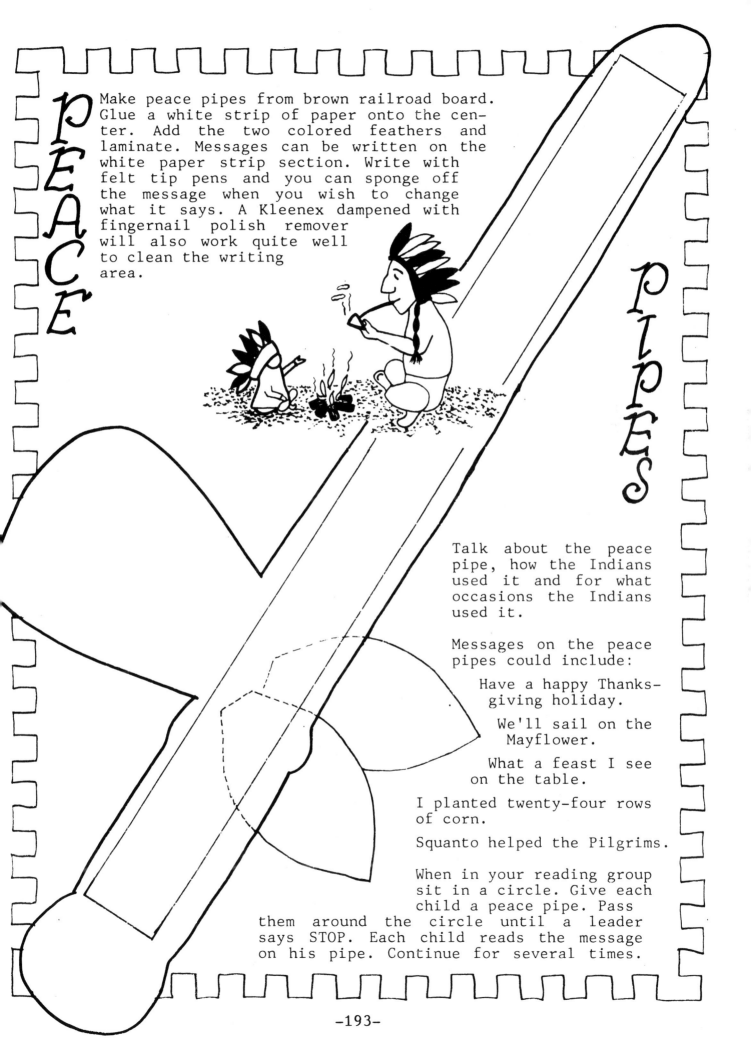

P
E
A
C
E

Make peace pipes from brown railroad board. Glue a white strip of paper onto the center. Add the two colored feathers and laminate. Messages can be written on the white paper strip section. Write with felt tip pens and you can sponge off the message when you wish to change what it says. A Kleenex dampened with fingernail polish remover will also work quite well to clean the writing area.

P
I
P
E
S

Talk about the peace pipe, how the Indians used it and for what occasions the Indians used it.

Messages on the peace pipes could include:

Have a happy Thanksgiving holiday.

We'll sail on the Mayflower.

What a feast I see on the table.

I planted twenty-four rows of corn.

Squanto helped the Pilgrims.

When in your reading group sit in a circle. Give each child a peace pipe. Pass them around the circle until a leader says STOP. Each child reads the message on his pipe. Continue for several times.

A PAPER BAG PUPPET

Here is a simple kind of puppet that any age child can make..even 4 and 5 year olds. Begin with a small brown paper bag. Add details with construction paper cut-outs and felt tip pens. The teacher will need to do the cutting for the smaller children.

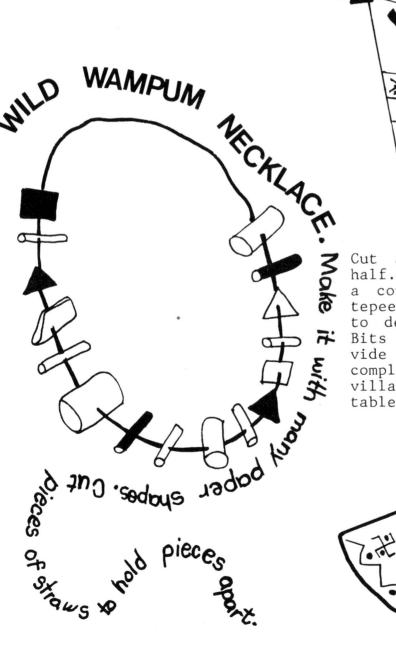

WILD WAMPUM NECKLACE. Make it with many paper shapes. Cut pieces of straws to hold pieces apart.

Cut a 12" brown circle in half. Form the ½ circle into a cone shape and a simple tepee is made. It is easier to decorate before shaping. Bits of toothpicks will provide the poles. Collect the complete ones and create a village on a large flat table.

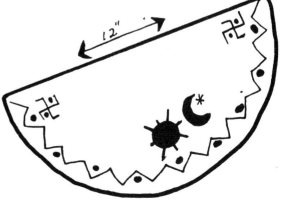

12"

PUPPETS

Fold a white piece of 9" x 12" construction paper into thirds. Cut a flesh-colored piece (for a Pilgrim) or a light brown-colored piece (for an Indian) in a circle, with a 5" diameter for the head. Cut it into 2/3 and 1/3. The larger piece will be glued to the top fold and the smaller one to the inside of the mouth opening. Fingers go into the top opening and the thumb in the bottom one. Hold puppet upright so it faces the front, then open and shut to TALK. We suggest the following poetry book for some very delightful poems. . .

THE GOLDEN FLUTE, an anthology of poetry for young children. Hubbard and Babbit. John Day Co., New York.
"Thanksgiving" by Margaret Munsterberg.
"Thanksgiving Day" by Lydia Maria Child.
"The Pilgrims Came" by Annette Wynne.
"There's a Big Fat Turkey" by unknown.

3"

12"

Also make this into a Pilgrim man or lady.

Pick a feather...

Make a Pilgrim puppet. Write: An Indian helped the Pilgrims. He was a friend. His name was Squanto. Draw 3 things you are thankful for. Draw an Indian. Draw 7 things the Pilgrims had for dinner. Write: See the Mayflower. It brought the Pilgrims to America. Write 5 of the sentence strips. Make one big turkey or 2 little ones. Play the teepee game. Write the Thanksgiving words. Make a turkey sandwich.

Cut 2 lengths of 3" x 22" RR board of orange, yellow, or brown for the headband. Cut another strip of the same color 1½" x 22" from the RR board to form the pocket behind the 3" strip. Tape the bottom edges and then tape the two strips together in the middle. Laminate entire strip.

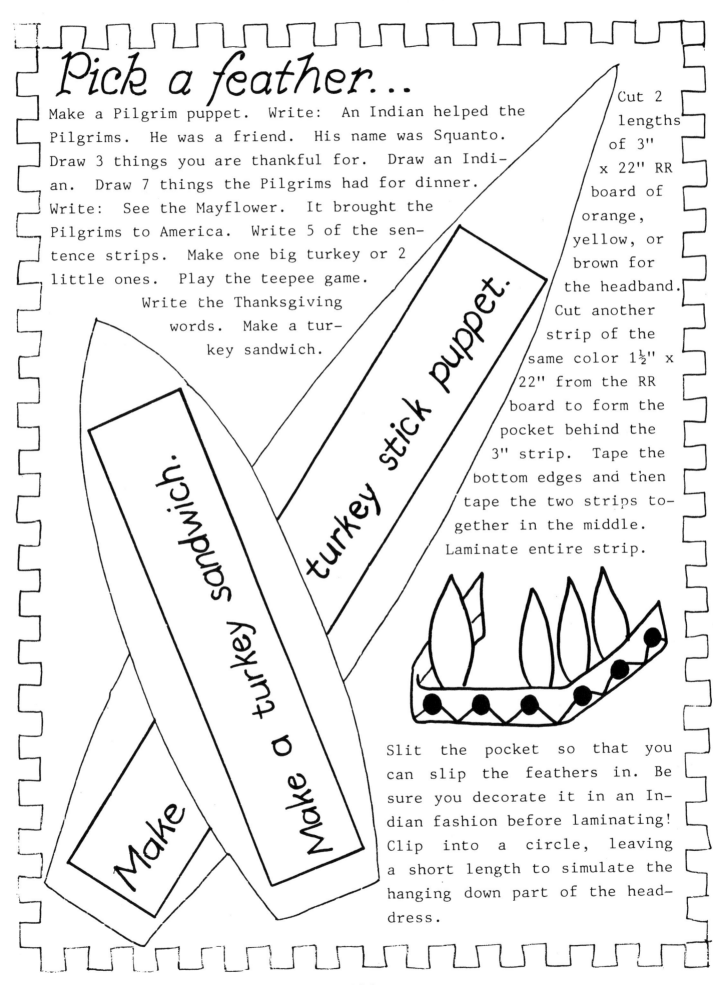

Make a turkey sandwich.

turkey stick puppet.

Make

Slit the pocket so that you can slip the feathers in. Be sure you decorate it in an Indian fashion before laminating! Clip into a circle, leaving a short length to simulate the hanging down part of the headdress.

RAIN DANCE

a fun relay...

Make another headdress like the one with the Indian tasks on it, or simply lay the feathers on two chairs at the head of each team.

Feathers are exactly like the task ones, of different sizes and colors. Here are the things to print on the feathers (glue a white strip in the middle of each feather to make the task stand out):

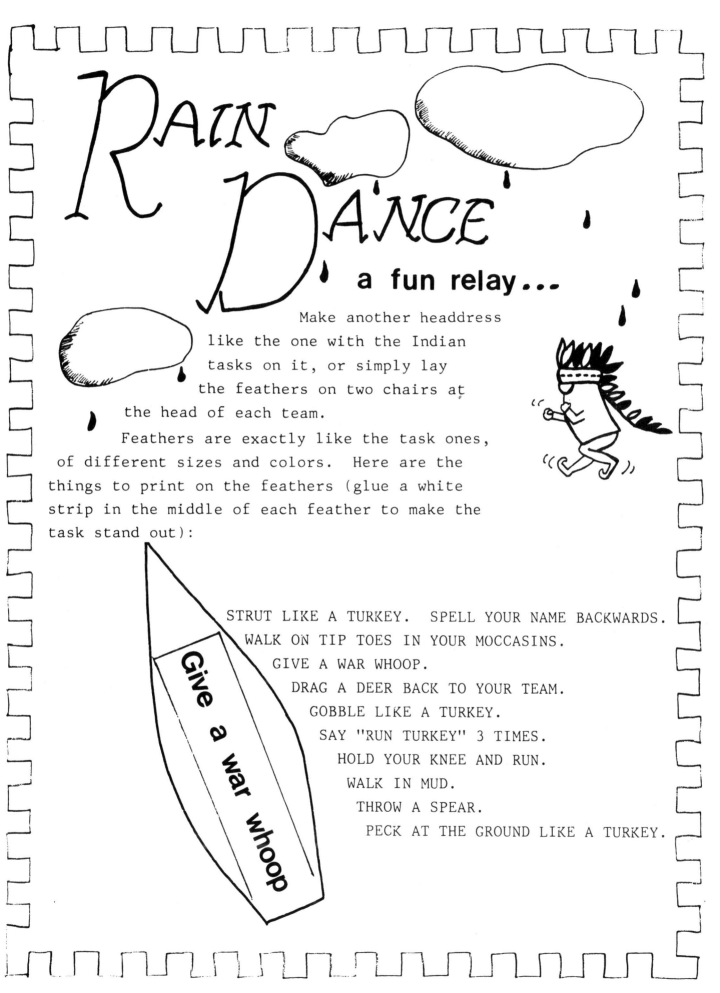

Give a war whoop

STRUT LIKE A TURKEY.   SPELL YOUR NAME BACKWARDS.

WALK ON TIP TOES IN YOUR MOCCASINS.

GIVE A WAR WHOOP.

DRAG A DEER BACK TO YOUR TEAM.

GOBBLE LIKE A TURKEY.

SAY "RUN TURKEY" 3 TIMES.

HOLD YOUR KNEE AND RUN.

WALK IN MUD.

THROW A SPEAR.

PECK AT THE GROUND LIKE A TURKEY.

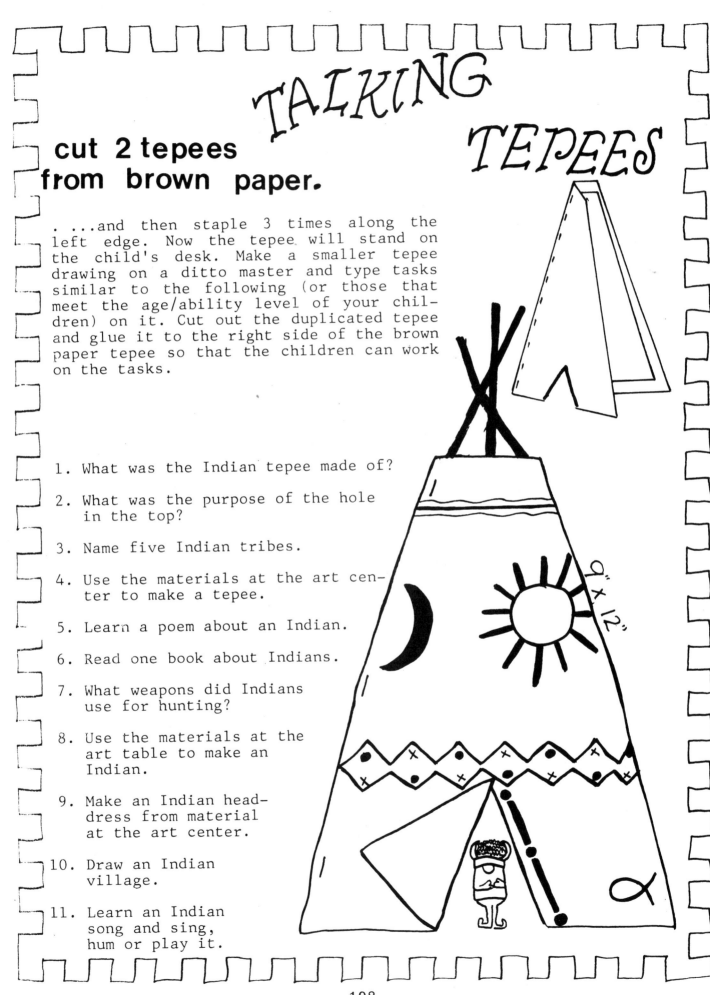

TALKING TEPEES

cut 2 tepees from brown paper.

. ...and then staple 3 times along the left edge. Now the tepee will stand on the child's desk. Make a smaller tepee drawing on a ditto master and type tasks similar to the following (or those that meet the age/ability level of your children) on it. Cut out the duplicated tepee and glue it to the right side of the brown paper tepee so that the children can work on the tasks.

1. What was the Indian tepee made of?

2. What was the purpose of the hole in the top?

3. Name five Indian tribes.

4. Use the materials at the art center to make a tepee.

5. Learn a poem about an Indian.

6. Read one book about Indians.

7. What weapons did Indians use for hunting?

8. Use the materials at the art table to make an Indian.

9. Make an Indian headdress from material at the art center.

10. Draw an Indian village.

11. Learn an Indian song and sing, hum or play it.

9" x 12"

TEPEES

THANKSGIVING

Make this tepee from brown railroad board. Make one for each letter in the word Thanksgiving. The letters are orange..add the brown top sticks and the sun and doorway detail. Then laminate. Now the children can manipulate these "letter tepees" to see how many words they can make from THANKSGIVING. This is a bit easier than just writing the big word at the top of a page..especially for the younger ones.

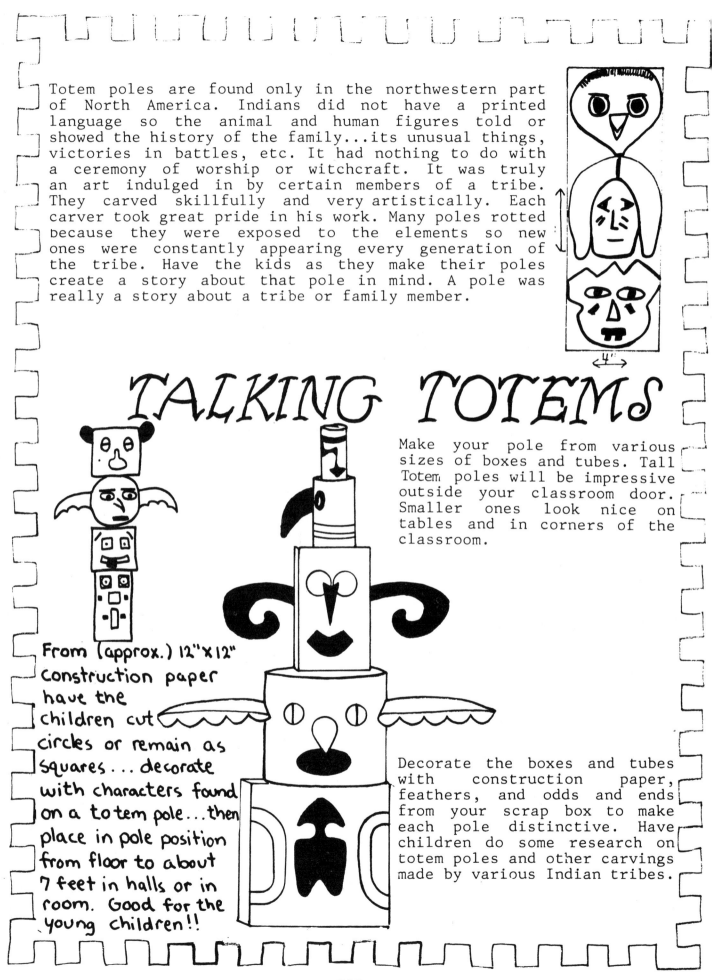

Totem poles are found only in the northwestern part of North America. Indians did not have a printed language so the animal and human figures told or showed the history of the family...its unusual things, victories in battles, etc. It had nothing to do with a ceremony of worship or witchcraft. It was truly an art indulged in by certain members of a tribe. They carved skillfully and very artistically. Each carver took great pride in his work. Many poles rotted because they were exposed to the elements so new ones were constantly appearing every generation of the tribe. Have the kids as they make their poles create a story about that pole in mind. A pole was really a story about a tribe or family member.

TALKING TOTEMS

Make your pole from various sizes of boxes and tubes. Tall Totem poles will be impressive outside your classroom door. Smaller ones look nice on tables and in corners of the classroom.

From (approx.) 12"x12" Construction paper have the children cut circles or remain as squares... decorate with characters found on a totem pole...then place in pole position from floor to about 7 feet in halls or in room. Good for the young children!!

Decorate the boxes and tubes with construction paper, feathers, and odds and ends from your scrap box to make each pole distinctive. Have children do some research on totem poles and other carvings made by various Indian tribes.

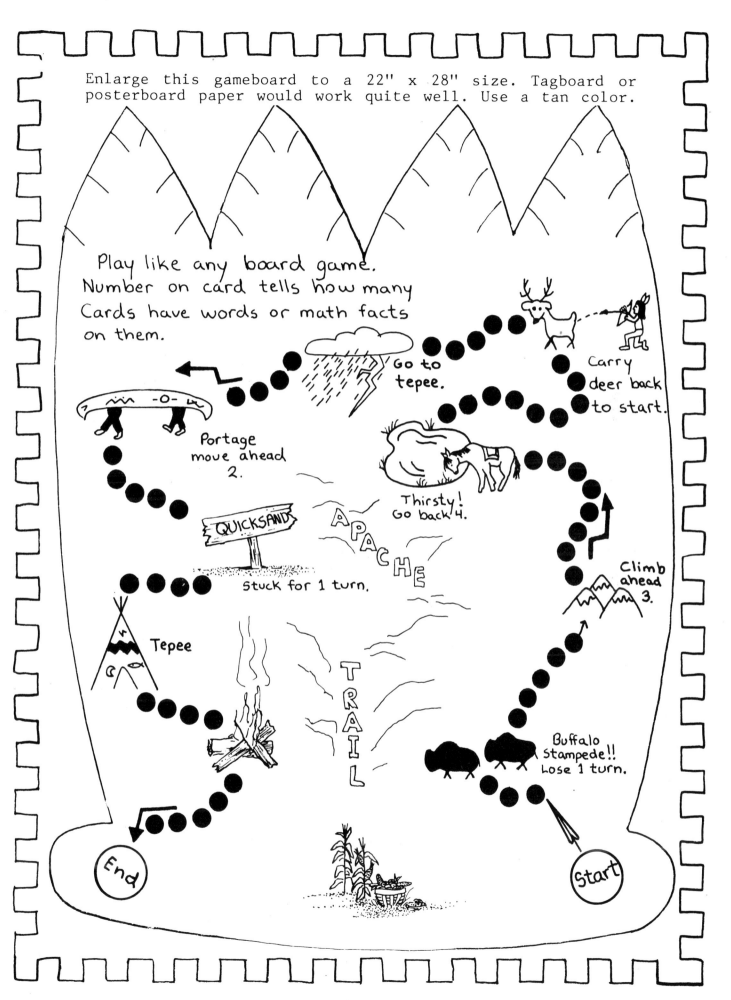

Enlarge this gameboard to a 22" x 28" size. Tagboard or posterboard paper would work quite well. Use a tan color.

Play like any board game. Number on card tells how many Cards have words or math facts on them.

Go to tepee.

Carry deer back to start.

Portage move ahead 2.

Thirsty! Go back 4.

QUICKSAND

APACHE

Stuck for 1 turn.

Climb ahead 3.

Tepee

TRAIL

Buffalo Stampede!! Lose 1 turn.

End

Start

TURKEY in the STRAW

LEARN song...

TURKEY IN THE STRAW ♪

Enlarge this picture to a 5" x 7" size. A bright color of tagboard can be used. Print Thanksgiving or Dolch words on the turkey.

Play HIDE THE CORN. Make a kernel of corn from yellow tagboard. Spread out the turkey cards, words up. One child hides the kernel as the other players close their eyes. Players open eyes and the child who hid the corn asks the others to find the kernel of corn. Players must be able to pronounce the word, then they can look under the turkey.

Find out what these INDIAN things are:

Indian root	Indian corn
Indian tobacco	Indian summer
Indian pipe	Indian meal
Indian turnip	Indian millet
Indian clubs	Indian territory
Indian file	Indian root
Indian red	Indiana

Name 10 tribes. Put them on a map of the U.S.A.

Name some famous chiefs or Indians.

Find out 5 things about turkeys.

tasks for cards

5"

7"

continued...

Make a paper fence from a sheet of white tagboard. Attach to a square or rectangle of styrofoam. Completed turkeys can be FENCED IN.

Cut the top of a 1/2 pint milk carton off. Cover sides with brown paper. Add colored loops to the back. Slip head into a slit in the front. This makes a nice container.

Cut brown paper strips 2" x 10". Form each into a loop. Cut various lengths of colored paper. Fill the inside of the back with loops. Make a slit for the neck and head in the front. These will make nice decorations for the family dinner table. If larger loops tend to fall over, glue several loops together.

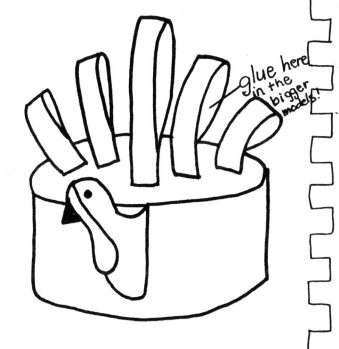

glue here in the bigger models!

folded edge

8" total

Fold a piece of brown or black paper (10" x 8") to a 10" x 4" size. Cut the strips across the fold. Be sure to leave peaks in a fold. When finished you may gently push the folds down into "not so stiff" tail feather shapes. Glue the head to the body by making a small tab at the base of the neck. Add wings in the same manner. Place a small nut cup inside.

Keep all those turkey gobblers in a good place! No matter which art turkey you choose to make, stand some of them inside this farm fence. The size of the fence should depend on the size of the turkeys you and your students make.

Make paper turkeys without feathers. Cut separate feathers. Children write a word on each one for each letter in Thanksgiving.

FENCE THEM IN

TO MAKE THE FENCE: Use good stiff white paper. Each piece should be about 9" x 12". Fold along the 12" side. Make four folds similar to those used to make a string of paper dolls. After you have a number of sections cut, tape them together into a rectangle or an oval corral.

If available, place yellow Easter grass or a little straw inside the fence.

Name _____

A TURKEY TRIP

1. I see _____ turkeys.

2. The turkeys are _____.
   big   little

3. The turkey's 👁's are _____.
   red   brown   black

4. Turkey 🪶's are _____.
   brown   black   orange

5. A turkey has _____ legs.

If possible visit a turkey farm. If not, maybe a turkey can visit your classroom. If the turkey is co-operative he may give his gobble for you. Can you distinguish between a hen and a gobbler's voice? For older children create an observation worksheet. List several questions for the students to answer while they are observing.

I can see a turkey.

Words 'n Wishbones

Use this wishbone as a pattern for your students. The first exercise asks them to simply complete the sentence. Next have students finish the wish pretending they were a famous person (Disney, Washington, Carter, Nixon, Mickey Mouse). Add other people from your school, including the principal. What would her wishes be?

Have students draw a picture of themselves with cartoon-like thinking clouds above their heads. In the clouds students need to add pictures of things that they wish for that cannot be bought. Put these wish posters on a bulletin board or on the classroom door.

Use areas of the blackboard to make wishbone lists. Students add to these categories:
-Shorter than a wishbone.
-Same size as a.....
-That has 2 parts like a wishbone.
-Things to make a wish on.....
-Things that are brittle....

Do week-long contests with two teams adding to lists.

Use the wishbone pattern as a bulletin board beginning. Cut letters that say, "I WISH YOU WOULD READ ONE OF THESE....". Have students draw pictures of their favorite book with the title at the bottom of the picture or have them draw first and then cut out the main character from their book. Add a paper wishbone next to each picture.

Scout your library for books about characters and their wishes to start students thinking. WISH AGAIN BIG BEAR by Richard Margolis, MacMillan,1972, and THE WISH AT THE TOP, by Chris Conover, Crowell, 1974, are good ones to begin with.

I WISH...

Prepare 13 cards with wishbones drawn on them as shown. On each card write a word that needs to be practiced. The word cards are spread, word-side up on the playing surface. Taking turns, players may pick up either 1, 2 or 3 wishbone cards if they can read the words on them. The person who ends up with an ODD number of cards wins the game. Because there are few cards in the game, make sure they contain words the kids need to practice.

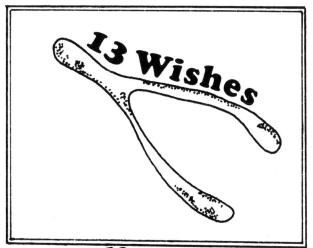

a reading thinking game

WISHBOOKS

Wishbones can be made simply by stapling half sheets of paper together. Have students copy the following sentences from the board. One sentence should be written at the bottom of each page. The task: finish the sentence and illustrate.

I wish.........
I wish I could.......
I wish it would........
I wish my teacher would...
I wish my friends would....

WISH-BONERS

A wish come true is a standard topic for creative writing. Give your youngsters an opportunity to write about wishes that came true and went wrong. Make certain to spend some time discussing possibilities before launching into the topic.

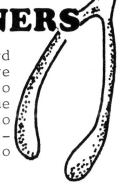

are wishes that went wrong

the SCOOP

Heritage of Flavor
a delightful FREE movie
Modern Talking Picture
Service
5000 Park Street N.
St. Petersburg, FL
33709

on CRANBERRIES

Buy different brands of cranberries..all kinds of varieties (sauce, relish).

Find all the numbers you can on the can label.

Where was it canned?

List all the words that describe cranberries.

Use paints, chalk, crayons. Can you make a cranberry color?

COLOR ME CRANBERRY

Do some research. Where are cranberries grown? On a map locate the areas. Where are cranberry products manufactured?

OPEN TO TASTE AFTER THE STUDY

How many words can you make from cranberry?

Describe a cranberry.

Taste one. Write words that tell how it tastes.

Crush cranberries and create juice. Does it make a good dye? Can you paint with it? Try. Add various amounts of water to some of the dye solution to make tints of the cranberry color. Fold paper napkins and dip the pointed ends into the various dye shades.

you'll Relish these!

American Indians discovered the cranberry. In 1810 it was grown as a crop. Write to the various companies that can cranberries for more information and pictures.

It's a **CRANBERRY** World

Create a bulletin board of all red. Cranberry people in a cranberry world.

Paint, color, cut and glue paper, all red of course. Red flowers, red buildings, red sky. It's a cranberry world.

Have children cut red circles. Discuss all the words that tell about cranberries (or Thanksgiving). Write the words on the chalkboard. Each child writes those that he knows how to read. Each should be printed on a cranberry. Give each child a piece of brown paper to make a box from. Each cranberry word can be glued to the box.

A 3# coffee can covered with white adhesive paper is the beginning of this project. Write math sets on it to suit your age level. The cranberries can be made from red tagboard. On these put the answer and a small piece of magnetic tape. Put an answer sheet inside the can to help settle disagreements and of course, the cranberries can also be stored inside. Be sure to make the squares before putting the paper on the can.

"Jelly" good fun!!

String Along

For a Christmas chain add white pieces in the shape of popcorn. Glue at intervals between the berries.

CRANBERRY

Write sentences or short poems in the bounce up and down pattern illustrated below!

b$_e$$_l$ow!

b o u n c e

CORN COUNTY
welcomes you to its

annual

Hang banner in room or across the hall.

Visit a grain elevator or a feed store. That is a great place to see <u>CORN</u>. Make a class collection. How many things can you find that are made from corn? Bring the actual items and pictures of items. Set up a display in the classroom.

Make a collection of corny jokes. Write each joke on a cob shape made of tagboard.

Grow some corn in the classroom. How fast does it grow? How large will it grow? Measure each day and keep growth records. The corn can be easily grown in empty milk cartons.

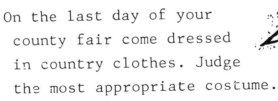

On the last day of your county fair come dressed in country clothes. Judge the most appropriate costume.

Get ears of corn from a farmer or an elevator and have an old fashioned corn shucking contest. Keep the kernels for winter feeding of birds.

If you start this unit in early fall eat fresh corn...boiled or roasted with melted butter and salt as a climax to this study.

SCARECROW SPECIAL

To complete this center you will need a scarecrow and a cassette tape recorder to make the scarecrow talk. Make your scarecrow from broomsticks which form a "T" shape and old clothing. Then, STUFF! Or, you could enlarge the drawing on this page. Touches of fabric and a little real straw will add just the right touch.

Then, tape—record the directions for the activities that follow on the next few pages. Add some of your own. Students will benefit from following oral directions.

PUPPETRY

12 " stick

6" yarn from stick to head

12 " yarn from stick to hand

A LA SCARECROW

Art projects are excellent for reinforcing the skill of following directions. The pattern for the pieces of this scarecrow puppet are found on the next page and should be cut from lightweight tagboard. Using fabric scraps, students dress their scarecrow. Join arms, legs and head to the body with brass fasteners. A light stick about 12 inches long controls the puppet. Students can work to the music from The Wizard of OZ, especially "If I Only Had a Brain".

brass fasteners

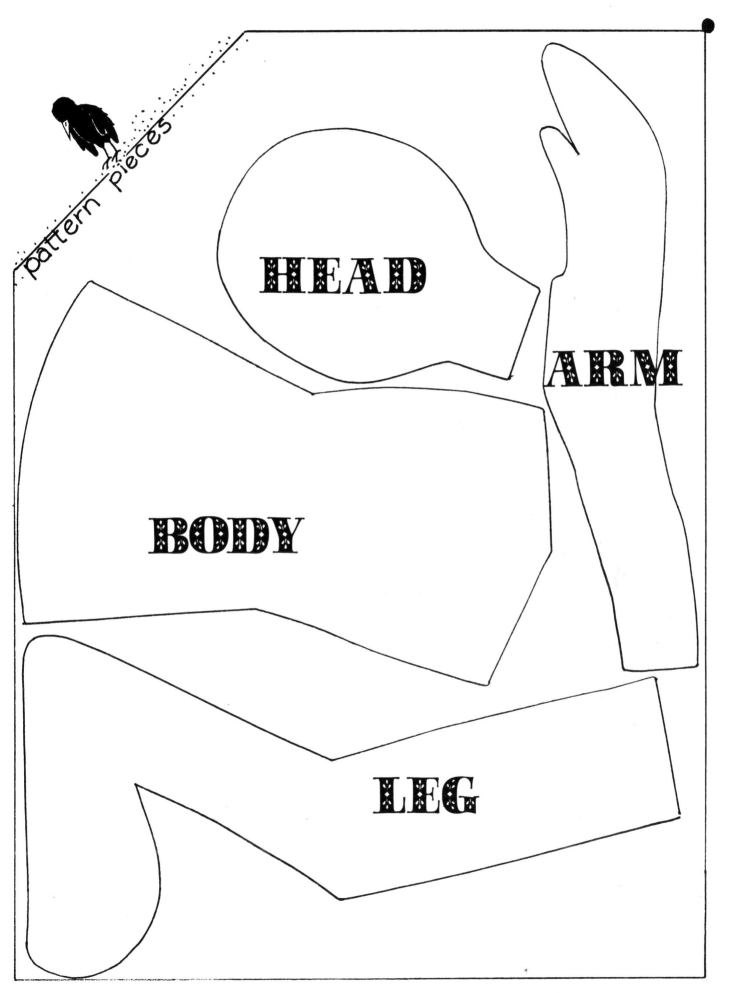

pattern pieces

HEAD

ARM

BODY

LEG

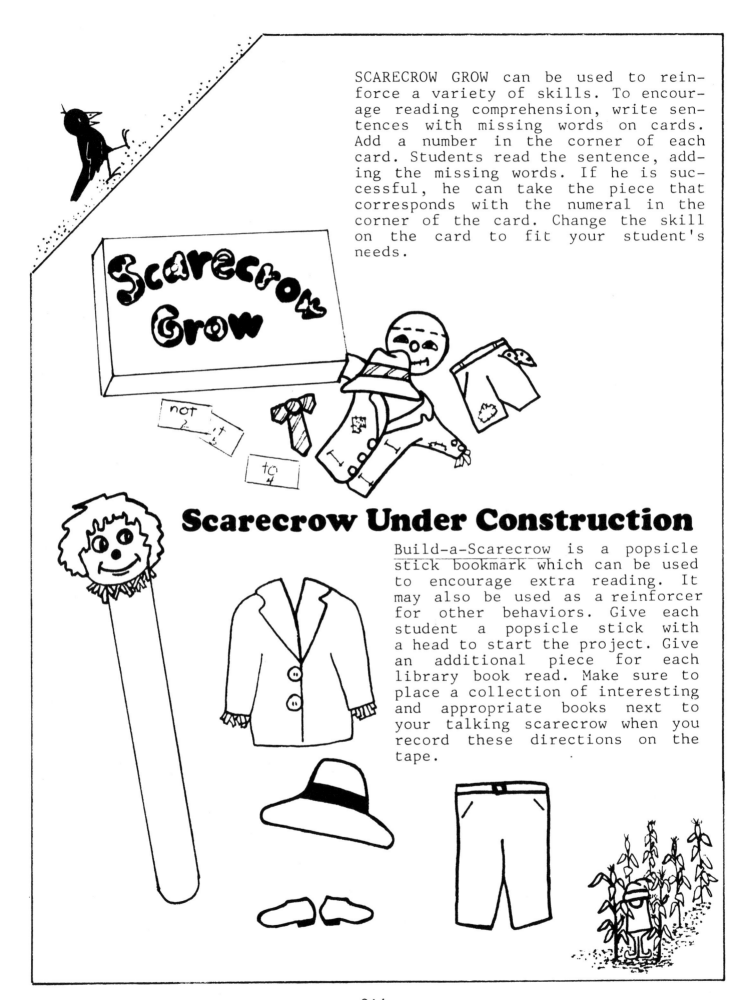

SCARECROW GROW can be used to reinforce a variety of skills. To encourage reading comprehension, write sentences with missing words on cards. Add a number in the corner of each card. Students read the sentence, adding the missing words. If he is successful, he can take the piece that corresponds with the numeral in the corner of the card. Change the skill on the card to fit your student's needs.

Scarecrow Under Construction

Build-a-Scarecrow is a popsicle stick bookmark which can be used to encourage extra reading. It may also be used as a reinforcer for other behaviors. Give each student a popsicle stick with a head to start the project. Give an additional piece for each library book read. Make sure to place a collection of interesting and appropriate books next to your talking scarecrow when you record these directions on the tape.

SCARECROW GROW!

Duplicate six copies of this page on six different color of construction paper. Cut the pieces apart and laminate. Prepare cards and store all pieces in a small box that has been covered with self-adhesive plastic.

Black paper crows hung near your scarecrow will give your room a cornfield realism. Students begin with a cylinder for the body and a cylinder for the head. Have them cut "v-shapes" from the ends of a rectangle to form the wings. Glue the wing rectangle to the top of the body cylinder to form. Add eyes, beak, feet and other details. Hang a sample near the work area to guide students who are younger or less able. Plastic craft eyes from a dime store would add a special touch.

Bye, Bye, Blackbird

Scarecrow Trim		
1		Draw one Draw the hat.
2		Draw two Add a head.
3		Draw three Add a jacket.
4		Draw four Add the pants.
5		Draw five Add the shoes.
6		Draw six Add any trim.

Prepare this game for use with any skill. Explain how to play the game on the taped directions. Prepare the board as shown. It can be placed on one side of a file folder with scrap paper in a pocket on the other side. Cut a stack of cards. On each card write the word or skill to be practiced. Add a small numeral in the corner of the card. To play, students must turn over a card and read the word. Students may add the detail which corresponds with the numeral. The first player to draw a complete scarecrow wins the game.

Here's a scarecrow to join your reading group.

HATS OFF!

Make a transparency from the scarecrow pattern on this page. On each arm, leg, head or other body part write a phonic skill. Cut a hat using this pattern from paper. The game is played like Pin the Tail on the Donkey. Students try to pin the hat on the head of the scarecrow. If the student puts the hat on one of the parts with the skill written, he must think of a word for that skill. For example, if the hat is placed on the arm where "br" is written the player must say a word that begins with "br".

Alternative: Write texture words about the scarecrow pattern. Duplicate a copy for each student. The task is to find appropriate fabric swatches and glue them in the proper places.

Use only the letters in the word SCARECROW
to find the words which match the definitions
listed below.

SCARECROW

1. Food that is not cooked is ___ ___ ___.

2. A measure of land ___ ___ ___ ___.

3. Sound of a rooster ___ ___ ___ ___.

4. Another name for automobiles ___ ___ ___ ___.

5. A mark left from a wound ___ ___ ___ ___.

6. A fight between nations ___ ___ ___.

7. What we do with clothes is ___ ___ ___ ___ them.

8. In order to ___ ___ ___ you must have a needle and thread.

9. A bow and ___ ___ ___ ___ ___.

10. An adult female hog ___ ___ ___.

11. To frighten is to ___ ___ ___ ___ ___.

12. To make a mistake is to ___ ___ ___.

Now can you think of two more?

_____

_____

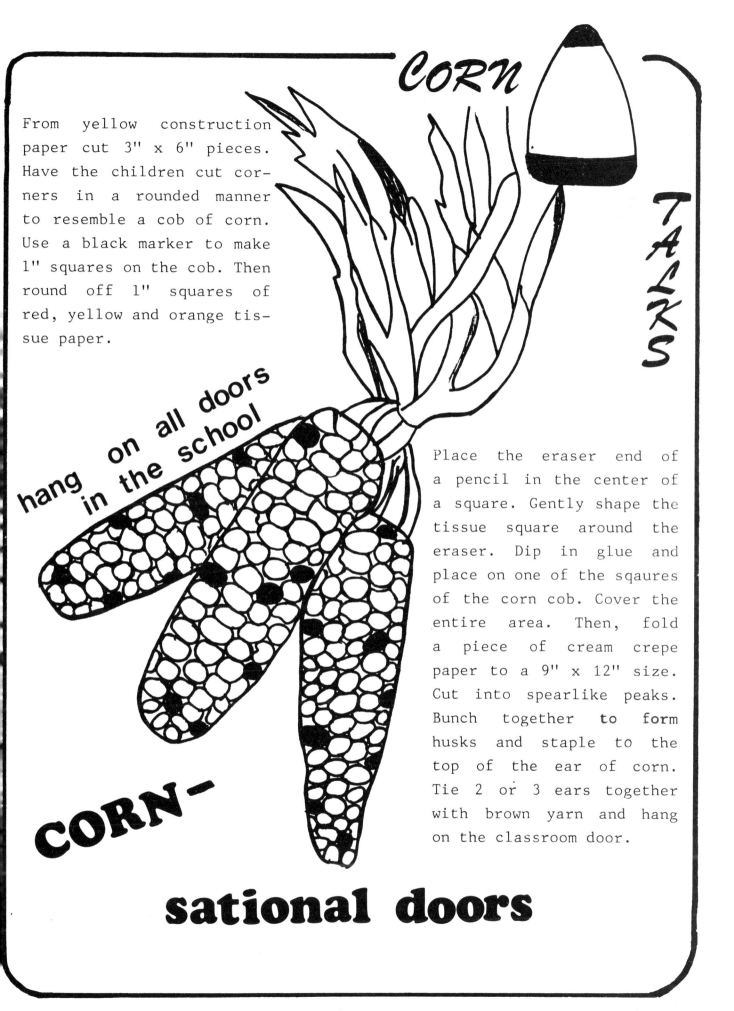

CORN TALKS

From yellow construction paper cut 3" x 6" pieces. Have the children cut corners in a rounded manner to resemble a cob of corn. Use a black marker to make 1" squares on the cob. Then round off 1" squares of red, yellow and orange tissue paper.

hang on all doors in the school

Place the eraser end of a pencil in the center of a square. Gently shape the tissue square around the eraser. Dip in glue and place on one of the sqaures of the corn cob. Cover the entire area. Then, fold a piece of cream crepe paper to a 9" x 12" size. Cut into spearlike peaks. Bunch together to form husks and staple to the top of the ear of corn. Tie 2 or 3 ears together with brown yarn and hang on the classroom door.

CORN- sational doors

OH SHUCKS

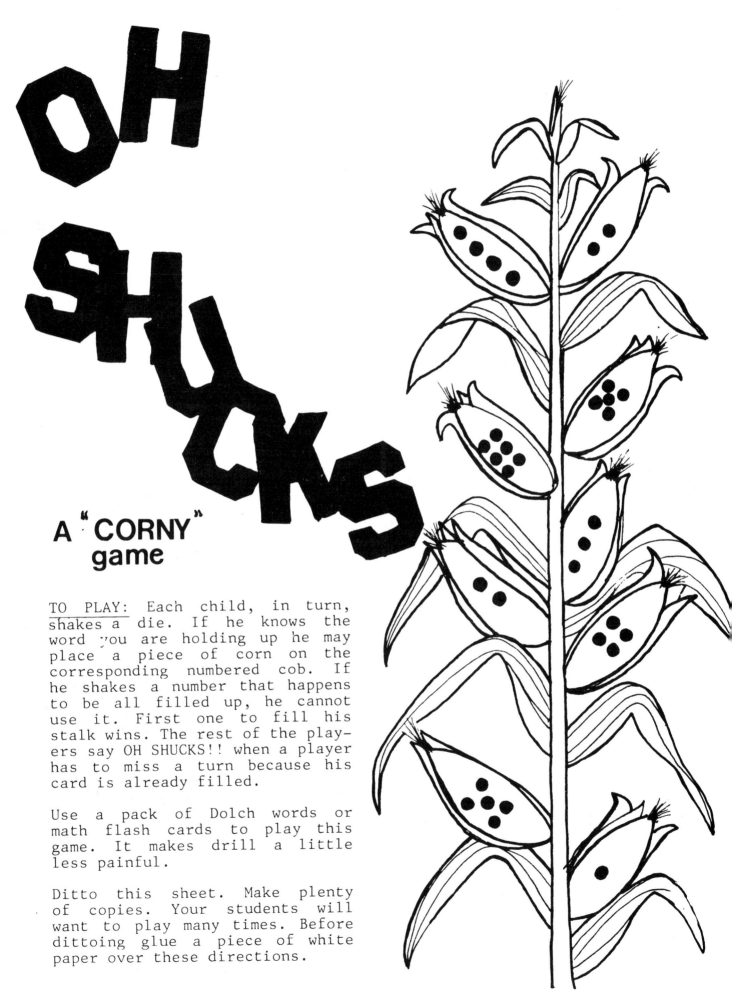

A "CORNY" game

TO PLAY: Each child, in turn, shakes a die. If he knows the word you are holding up he may place a piece of corn on the corresponding numbered cob. If he shakes a number that happens to be all filled up, he cannot use it. First one to fill his stalk wins. The rest of the players say OH SHUCKS!! when a player has to miss a turn because his card is already filled.

Use a pack of Dolch words or math flash cards to play this game. It makes drill a little less painful.

Ditto this sheet. Make plenty of copies. Your students will want to play many times. Before dittoing glue a piece of white paper over these directions.

To make the corn palaces, glue various colors of kernels of corn. Indian corn works well if it is available.

CORN PALACES...

Cover the bottom half of a milk carton with brown construction paper. Add the roof being sure to leave a bit of an overhang. Use the corn that is left over from your corn shucking contest to make these corn palaces. Glue two milk cartons together to make a bigger building.

CORN-NIBBLERS

CORN BREAD

1 cup flour, sifted
¼ cup sugar
4 tsp. baking powder
3/4 tsp. salt
1 cup cornmeal
2 eggs
1 cup milk
¼ cup shortening

MIX dry ingredients in above order, add eggs, milk and shortening. Put in a square pan. Bake at 425 degrees for 20 to 25 minutes.

CORNSTACKS (Haystacks)

2 pkgs. butterscotch bits
1 can chow mein noodles
1 can of peanuts

1. Put the butterscotch bits in a pan and melt.

2. Stir in the peanuts

3. Stir in chow mein

4. Drop a teaspoon of mixture onto wax paper. Eat and enjoy!

Cook up the REAL thing. Boil ears of corn or cook them on a grill. Incorporate some math fun. How many bits per ear of corn? How many kernels in the average bite? How long does it take to eat an ear of corn?

Brazil nut

pecan

macademia

'Tis a NUTTY thing to do

You will need to plan for this unit well in advance to assure yourself of the availability of all the nuts, whether from trees or from the store. Nuts seem to be readily available around the holiday season.

Present a warm brown wooden bowl full of all the types of nuts you will be studying. As you study each nut, be sure each child has one to hold, crack and taste.

As each child holds the nut you are studying for the day, look at the color. What words describe the color? How does the shell feel? Is it rough, smooth, bumpy, fuzzy? Smell the shell. Try to crack it between your fingers. Use nutcrackers or find small hammers to open the shell. Continue the investigation of the nut. What does it look like? What does it feel like? What is the smell? What words can be used to describe the taste?

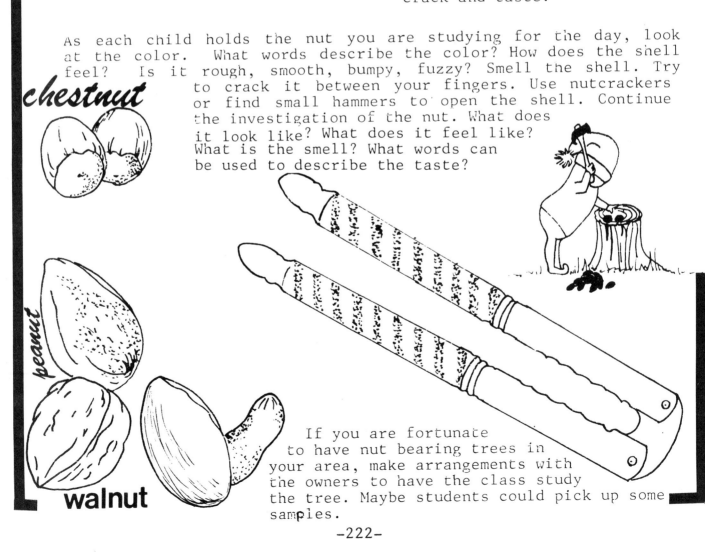

chestnut

peanut

walnut

If you are fortunate to have nut bearing trees in your area, make arrangements with the owners to have the class study the tree. Maybe students could pick up some samples.

in a NUT SHELL

Research and discuss......
What is the food value of nuts? Why are they good for us?

Name some trees that have nuts as seeds.

Write 15 words that describe nuts.... oily, smooth, firm.

Write tasks similar to those listed on this page on 3" x 5" index cards. Glue a nut shell on each card. Place the cards in your "nutty" learning center.

Find words in the dictionary that contain the letters "nut". The person with the longest list gets a small bag of peanuts.

How many different kinds of nuts can the students name?

Listen to the "Nutcracker Suite". Have students draw a picture of the Nutcracker as they listen.

TASK CARD SHAPE

it's the
PE A NU T-Tiest !!

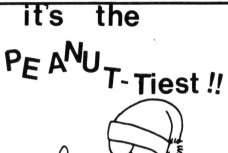

1 cup (6 oz.) semi-sweet choc. bits
1 cup (6 oz.) butterscotch bits
1 can Borden Eagle Brand Sweetened
     Condensed Milk (not evaporated)
1 cup coarsely chopped nuts
½ teaspoon vanilla

Melt choc. and butterscotch bits with the sweetened milk over a warm burner. Stir carefully so it doesn't burn. When melted, remove from heat, add nuts and vanilla. Blend well. Chill until mixture is thickened.

Gather a variety of brands of peanut butter. Have a taste contest, just like on TV. Which tastes the "peanuttiest"?

Make a graph of how many can identify each brand.

the NUTT-iest !

COCONUT-cracker

Melt 8 oz. of chocolate chips over low ½ heat. Take pan off the stove and add ½ pound of peanuts (Spanish). Stir it well. Drop by spoonfuls onto waxed paper. Chill in the refrigerator.

NUT BALLS

Place graham crackers in a pan. Sprinkle one teaspoon of brown sugar on each. Put ½ teaspoon butter on the sugar. Put one tablespoon coconut on top of the butter. Put under the broiler until the coconut is browned and the butter melted. Y*U*M*M*Y!

Buy a long white cake or an angel food cake. Cut into small squares. Frost all sides of the squares lightly and roll in finely chopped peanuts.

COME AND EAT

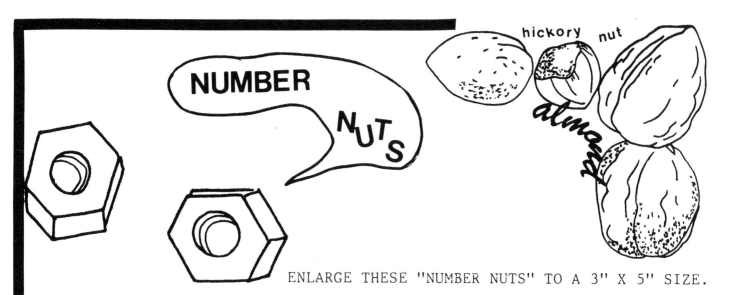

NUMBER NUTS

hickory nut

almond

acorn

hazelnut

ENLARGE THESE "NUMBER NUTS" TO A 3" X 5" SIZE.

Draw them onto a ditto master. Duplicate on a stiff kind of paper (light tagboard or construction paper). Print related math facts similar to the following on each.

1 minute = _____ seconds

2 hours = _____ minutes

½ hour = _____ minutes

180 minutes = _____ hours

etc.

1 pound = _____ ounces

2 dozen = _____

1 quart = _____ pints

2 gallons = _____ quarts

etc.

50¢ = _____ nickels

$1.00 = _____ pennies

25¢ = ____ dimes ____ nickels

$5.00 = _____ half dollars

etc.

1 month = ___ days

1 year = ___ days

60 days = ___ months

½ year = ___ days

etc.

Tie each group of completed "math nuts" together and send home so the child can show his parents and be proud.

coconut

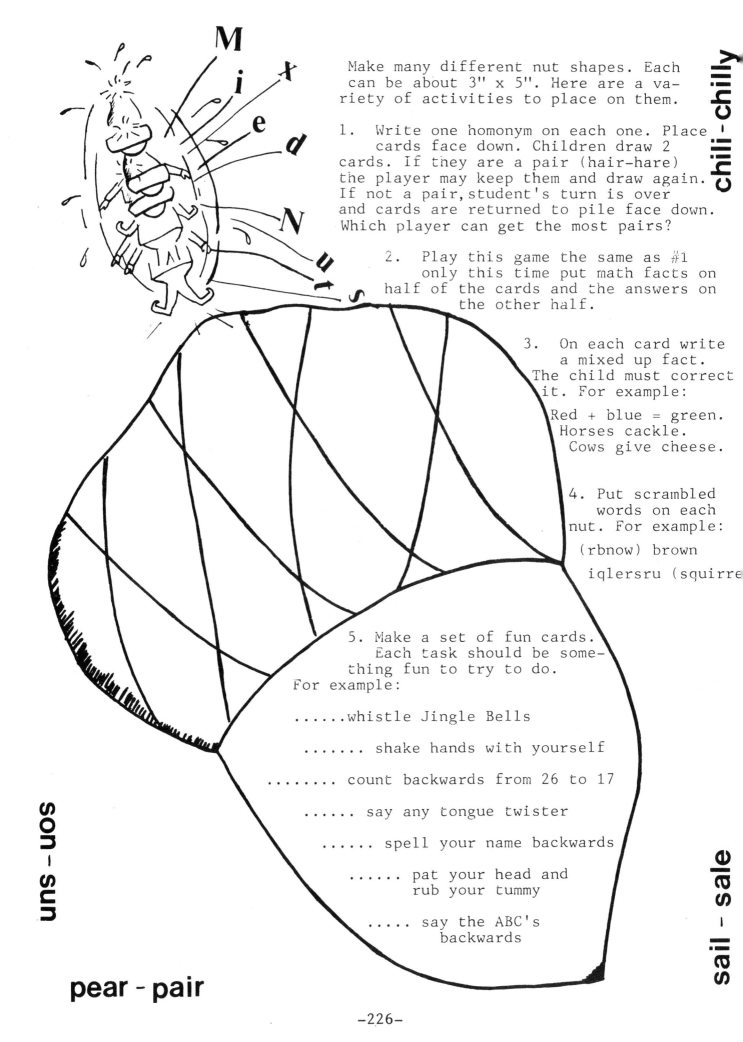

Mixed Nuts

Make many different nut shapes. Each can be about 3" x 5". Here are a variety of activities to place on them.

1. Write one homonym on each one. Place cards face down. Children draw 2 cards. If they are a pair (hair-hare) the player may keep them and draw again. If not a pair, student's turn is over and cards are returned to pile face down. Which player can get the most pairs?

2. Play this game the same as #1 only this time put math facts on half of the cards and the answers on the other half.

3. On each card write a mixed up fact. The child must correct it. For example:

Red + blue = green.
Horses cackle.
Cows give cheese.

4. Put scrambled words on each nut. For example:

(rbnow) brown

iqlersru (squirre

5. Make a set of fun cards. Each task should be something fun to try to do. For example:

......whistle Jingle Bells

.... shake hands with yourself

.... count backwards from 26 to 17

...... say any tongue twister

...... spell your name backwards

...... pat your head and
rub your tummy

..... say the ABC's
backwards

pear - pair

Vegetable Ventures

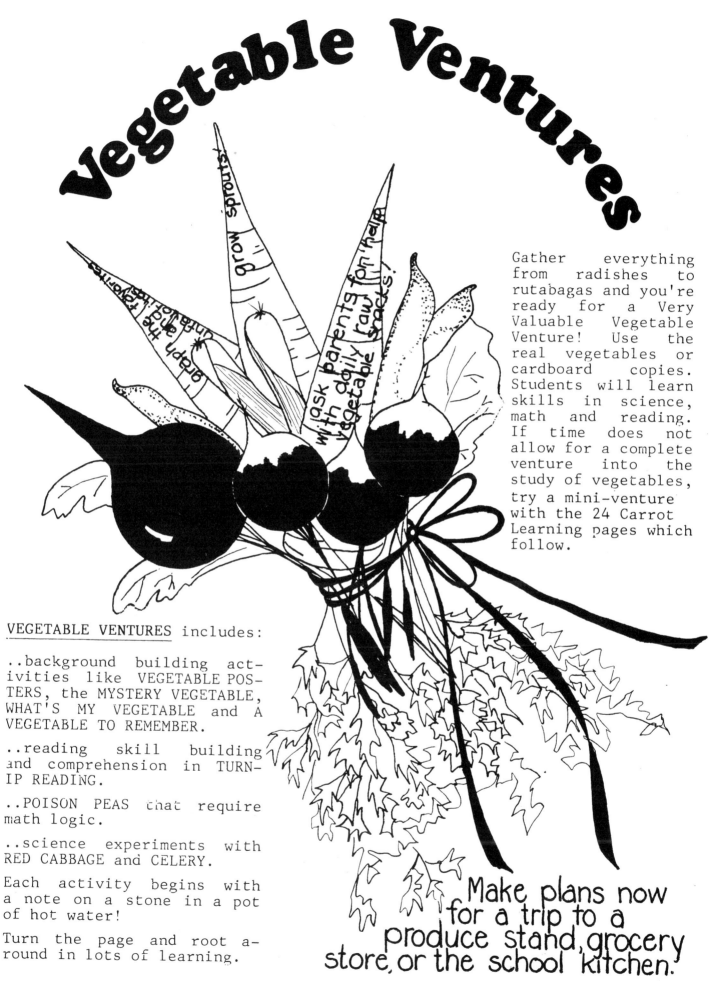

grow sprouts

graph and interpret vegetable taste tests

ask parents for help with daily raw vegetable snacks!

Gather everything from radishes to rutabagas and you're ready for a Very Valuable Vegetable Venture! Use the real vegetables or cardboard copies. Students will learn skills in science, math and reading. If time does not allow for a complete venture into the study of vegetables, try a mini-venture with the 24 Carrot Learning pages which follow.

VEGETABLE VENTURES includes:

..background building activities like VEGETABLE POSTERS, the MYSTERY VEGETABLE, WHAT'S MY VEGETABLE and A VEGETABLE TO REMEMBER.

..reading skill building and comprehension in TURNIP READING.

..POISON PEAS that require math logic.

..science experiments with RED CABBAGE and CELERY.

Each activity begins with a note on a stone in a pot of hot water!

Turn the page and root around in lots of learning.

Make plans now for a trip to a produce stand, grocery store, or the school kitchen!

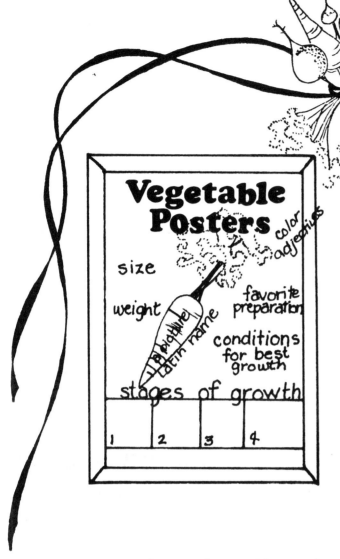

Vegetable posters provide the seeds for teaching this unit about vegetables as well as developing writing skills. Begin by brainstorming with the students about what things are important to know about vegetables. Make a list that includes descriptive adjectives about the color, shape and texture as well as the Latin names, best growing conditions, stages of growth and the best uses for the vegetables. Students select a vegetable, research the information and write it creatively on a poster. Information can also be illustrated. When the posters are done, hang them about the classroom. Using only the information shown on the posters, students write a brief report (perhaps the copy for a seed packet or catalog information) about one vegetable. Each report should consist only of one well written paragraph. With proper brainstorming and fact-gathering, a clear paragraph should be an achievable challenge. Combine all of the paragraphs into a vegetable booklet but keep it away from the hamster cage. It may be just good enough to eat.

POISON PEAS is a simple and quickly played math logic game. Make a pod from green paper as shown. Add twelve paper peas and ONE kernel of corn. Players take turns selecting either one or two peas. The player forced to take the kernel of corn loses the game.

POISON PEAS

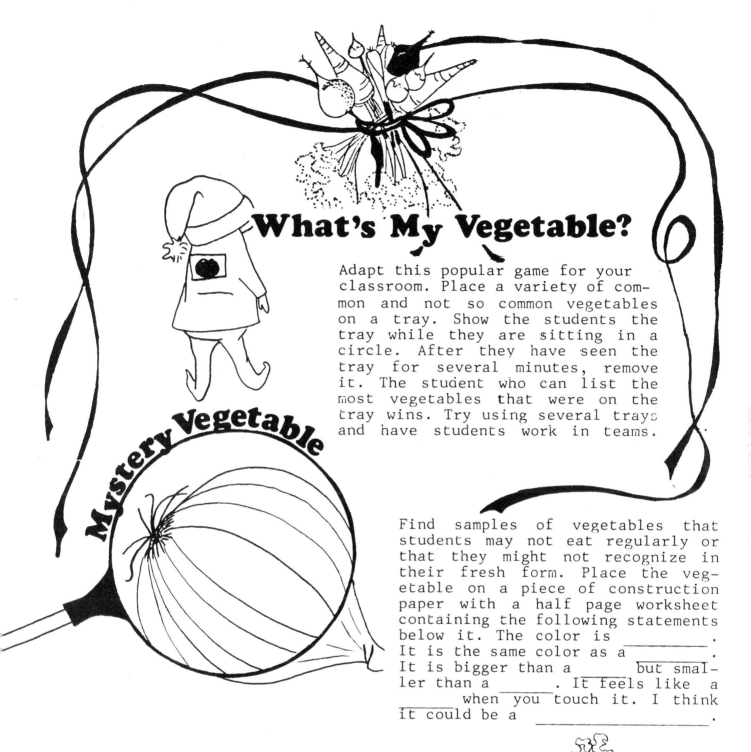

What's My Vegetable?

Adapt this popular game for your classroom. Place a variety of common and not so common vegetables on a tray. Show the students the tray while they are sitting in a circle. After they have seen the tray for several minutes, remove it. The student who can list the most vegetables that were on the tray wins. Try using several trays and have students work in teams.

Mystery Vegetable

Find samples of vegetables that students may not eat regularly or that they might not recognize in their fresh form. Place the vegetable on a piece of construction paper with a half page worksheet containing the following statements below it. The color is _____ .
It is the same color as a _____ .
It is bigger than a _____ but smaller than a _____ . It feels like a _____ when you touch it. I think it could be a _____ .

A Vegetable To Remember

Adapt this party game to vegetables and help children think about the attributes and categories of vegetables. Using a seed catalog, cut and pin one picture of a vegetable to the back of each student. The student may not know the name of his vegetable or see its picture. He may ask others a yes or no question to help him determine the vegetable's identity. The first 10 children to guess their vegetable get a FRESH CARROT.

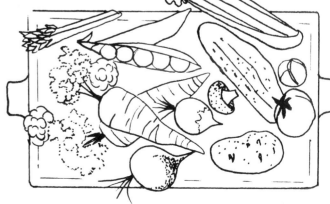

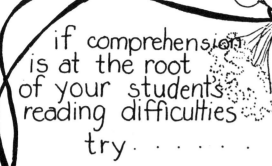

if comprehension
is at the root
of your students
reading difficulties
try . . . . .

Turn-ip Reading

Adapt this bingo-style learning game for a variety of reading levels by changing the words or categories. Students take turns turning over a card, reading it, and covering their appropriate square with a lima bean. The first to cover all four corners or the entire card is the winner.

Words To Use

Use any of the following words or words which can be adjusted to the skill and interest of your students. Write the words on small 2" x 3" cards.

dandelion	automobile	scooter	basement	shamrock
own	stars	tiger	car	glass
pillow	blanket	bicycle	wagon	truck
van	radio	boy	girl	paper
card	boat	pencil	crayon	radish
bubble	gum	tar	spinach	sky
eyes	sheet	bird	music	tree
attic	pickle	trash	spark	puppy

Categories To Use

Use the following categories, or ones of your own to fit the abilities or background of your students. Write the categories on the chalkboard. Students fill in their turnip board with randomly placed categories.

SOMETHING: to eat, ride on, hide in, that barks, that flies, that sings, that burns, that's hard, with four corners, sparkling, wet, to play with, fuzzy, dangerous, deep, old, tiny, to write on, sticky, or easy to do.

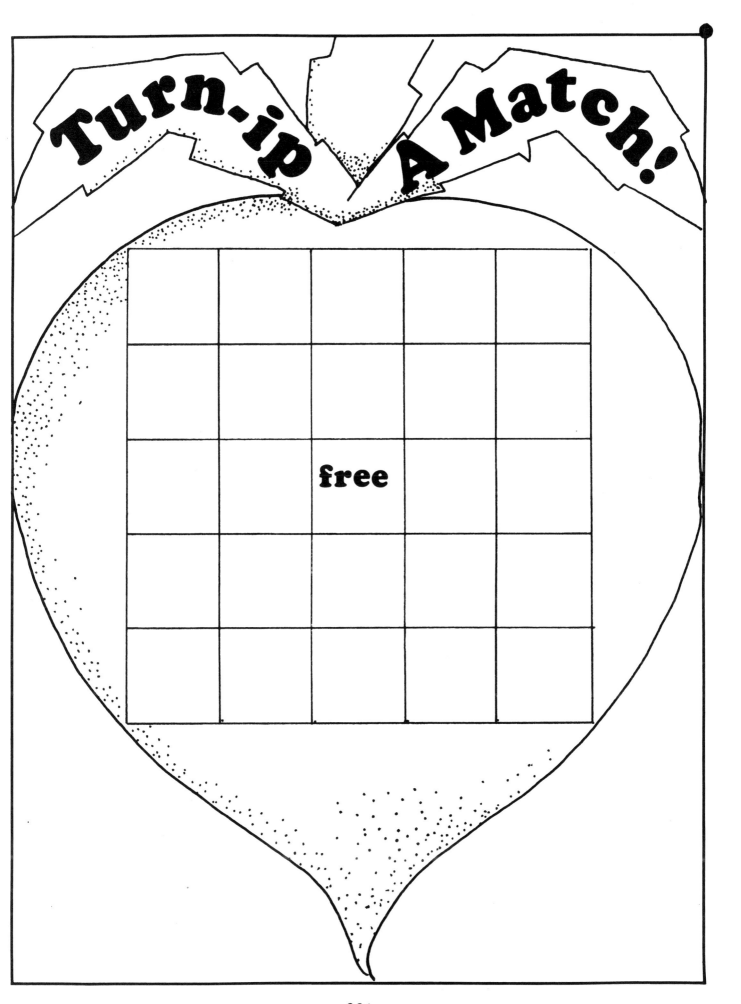

free

ideas to whet their appetites . . .
for learning!

Vegetable Soup

LET-TUCE launch a unit of study after scouring the library for the bushel of recource books and films-strips which are available. The U.S. Department of Agriculture has in the past had an excellent collection of materials on nutrition available for little or no cost.

The story of "STONE SOUP" can't be "BEET" for launching student interest in a unit on vegetables. A day or two before you read the story, write the following message on a large rock. Use permanent marker to write the message.

" ON _____ WE WILL READ A STORY ABOUT 2 SOLDIERS

WHO WERE IN A LOT OF HOT WATER!!!   BRING A VEGETABLE

THIS DAY AND ENJOY A MOUTH-WATERING STORY."

Put the rock in the kettle of water and place it where it can't be missed. Add a sign next to the kettle which says:

"COMING SOON.........CAN YOU GUESS?"

After enjoying the story make your own soup with the vegetables brought in by the children. Keep a chalkboard list of all the vegetables contributed. Make another list of all the vegetables NOT brought. Use one of the vegetables NOT brought in, and one perhaps students didn't even think of for the MYSTERY VEGETABLE exercise.

make plans now for a field trip to

farmers market, produce stand, grocery store or school district kitchen!

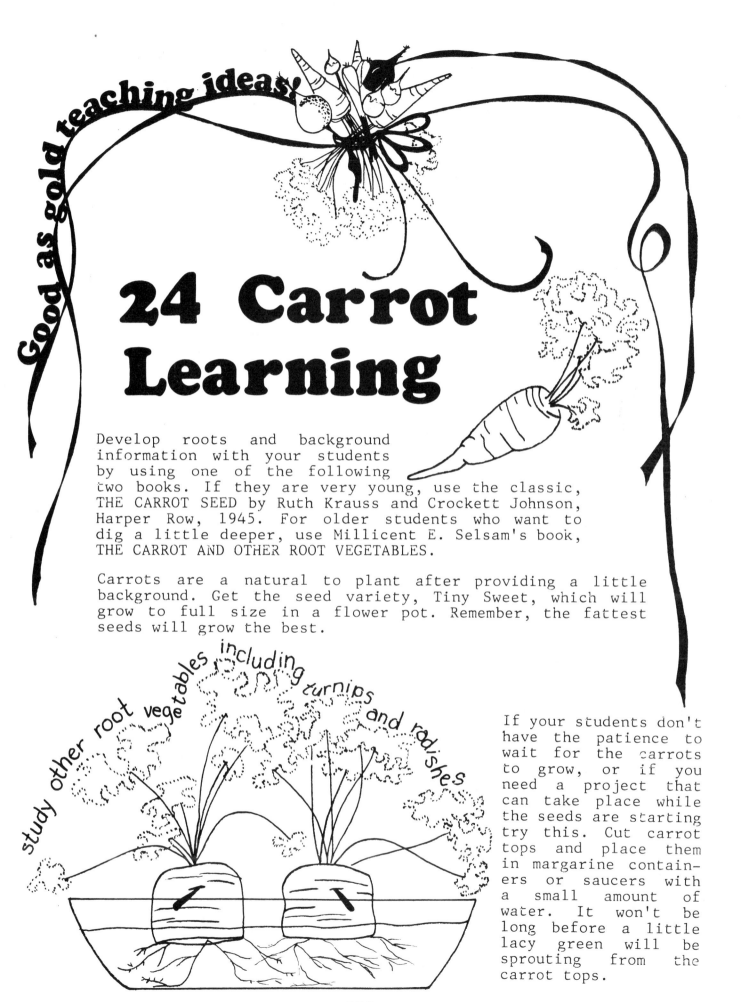

24 Carrot Learning

Develop roots and background information with your students by using one of the following two books. If they are very young, use the classic, THE CARROT SEED by Ruth Krauss and Crockett Johnson, Harper Row, 1945. For older students who want to dig a little deeper, use Millicent E. Selsam's book, THE CARROT AND OTHER ROOT VEGETABLES.

Carrots are a natural to plant after providing a little background. Get the seed variety, Tiny Sweet, which will grow to full size in a flower pot. Remember, the fattest seeds will grow the best.

study other root vegetables including turnips and radishes

If your students don't have the patience to wait for the carrots to grow, or if you need a project that can take place while the seeds are starting try this. Cut carrot tops and place them in margarine containers or saucers with a small amount of water. It won't be long before a little lacy green will be sprouting from the carrot tops.

Comic Carrots

COMICS ON CARROTS: To reinforce sequence, cut out several of the children's favorite comics from the Sunday paper. Put each of the panels on a separate paper carrot. Students should sort the carrots out and try to rearrange the comic strip in the proper sequence. You might also use sentences from a simple fairy tale for young children. For younger children use paragraphs from a newspaper story.

to the . . . Carrot Top!

To make this measuring gameboard cut a large carrot shape from orange cardboard. Mark each of the two long edges in either metric or inch measurements. Prepare a set of cards which say ½ inch ahead, back one inch, etc. Each of the two players turn over a card and move their markers along the ruled edge according to the directions given on the cards they draw. First to the carrot top wins.

Try Carrot Clutch' and the task card carrots on page 119 of Spring Surprises!

Cowboys and other Carrotures

A fun bulletin board and good seatwork activity begins with a stack of orange paper cut in rectangles. Have students cut the rectangles to look like carrots. Students then add distinguishing details which will turn their carrot into their favorite or most current book carrot. Mount on a bulletin board with the sign, "WE LIKE THESE CHARACTERS A WHOLE BUNCH".

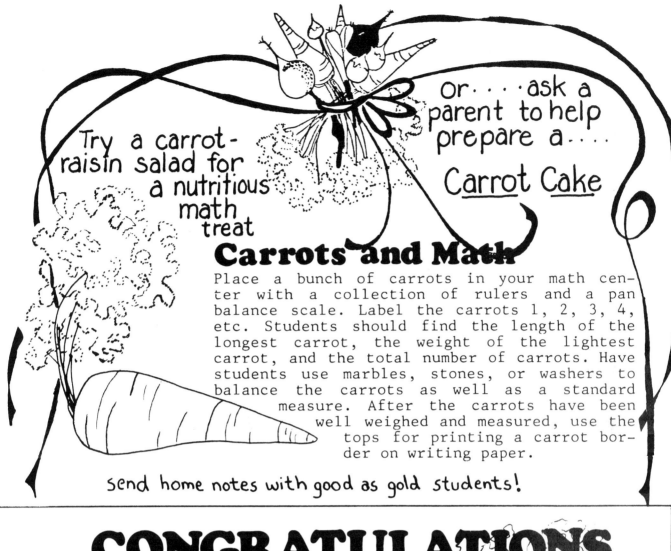

Try a carrot-raisin salad for a nutritious math treat

Or....ask a parent to help prepare a....

Carrot Cake

Carrots and Math

Place a bunch of carrots in your math center with a collection of rulers and a pan balance scale. Label the carrots 1, 2, 3, 4, etc. Students should find the length of the longest carrot, the weight of the lightest carrot, and the total number of carrots. Have students use marbles, stones, or washers to balance the carrots as well as a standard measure. After the carrots have been well weighed and measured, use the tops for printing a carrot border on writing paper.

Send home notes with good as gold students!

CONGRATULATIONS

You've done a ....

24 Carrot

job!

To _____

_____

_____

From _____

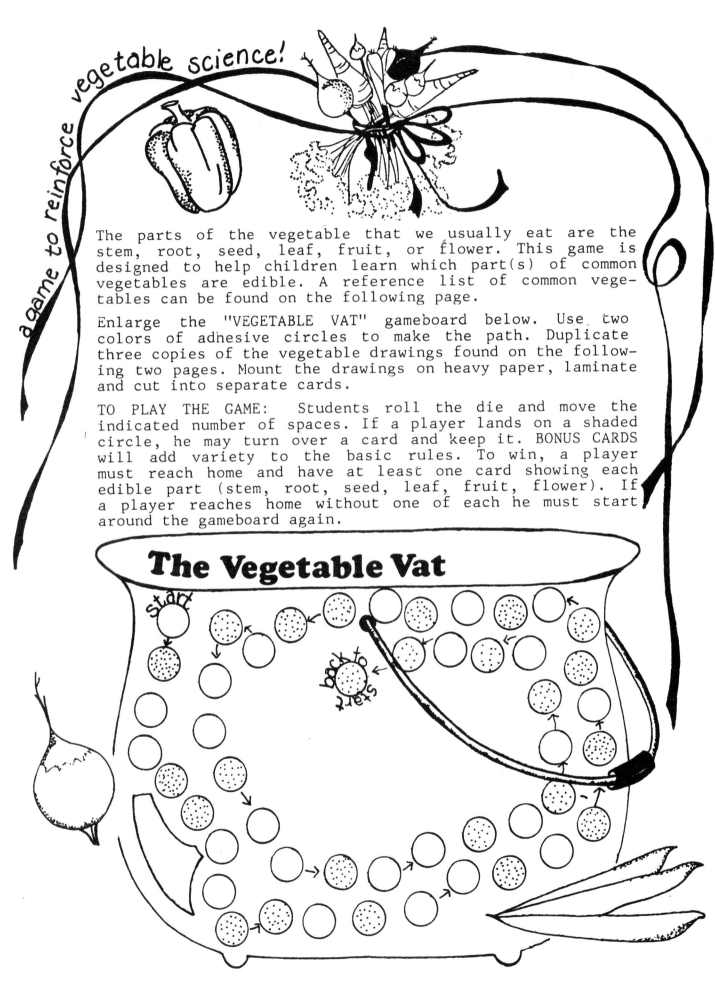

a game to reinforce vegetable science!

The parts of the vegetable that we usually eat are the stem, root, seed, leaf, fruit, or flower. This game is designed to help children learn which part(s) of common vegetables are edible. A reference list of common vegetables can be found on the following page.

Enlarge the "VEGETABLE VAT" gameboard below. Use two colors of adhesive circles to make the path. Duplicate three copies of the vegetable drawings found on the following two pages. Mount the drawings on heavy paper, laminate and cut into separate cards.

TO PLAY THE GAME: Students roll the die and move the indicated number of spaces. If a player lands on a shaded circle, he may turn over a card and keep it. BONUS CARDS will add variety to the basic rules. To win, a player must reach home and have at least one card showing each edible part (stem, root, seed, leaf, fruit, flower). If a player reaches home without one of each he must start around the gameboard again.

The Vegetable Vat

start

back to start

more vegetable vat!

Use the following resource list to help you prepare "THE VEGETABLE VAT" game. The list could also be turned into a guide chart for student use.

STEM

asparagas
celery
rhubarb

FRUIT

tomato
squash
pepper
pumpkin
cucumber
zucchini
egg plant

SEED

peas
corn
beans

FLOWER

cauliflower
broccoli

ROOT

turnip
radish
carrot
beet
onion

LEAF

lettuce
spinach
cabbage
Brussels sprouts

Pumpkin

Cucumber

Zucchini

Peas

Egg Plant

Bonus draw again

Okra

Cauliflower

Have Fun!

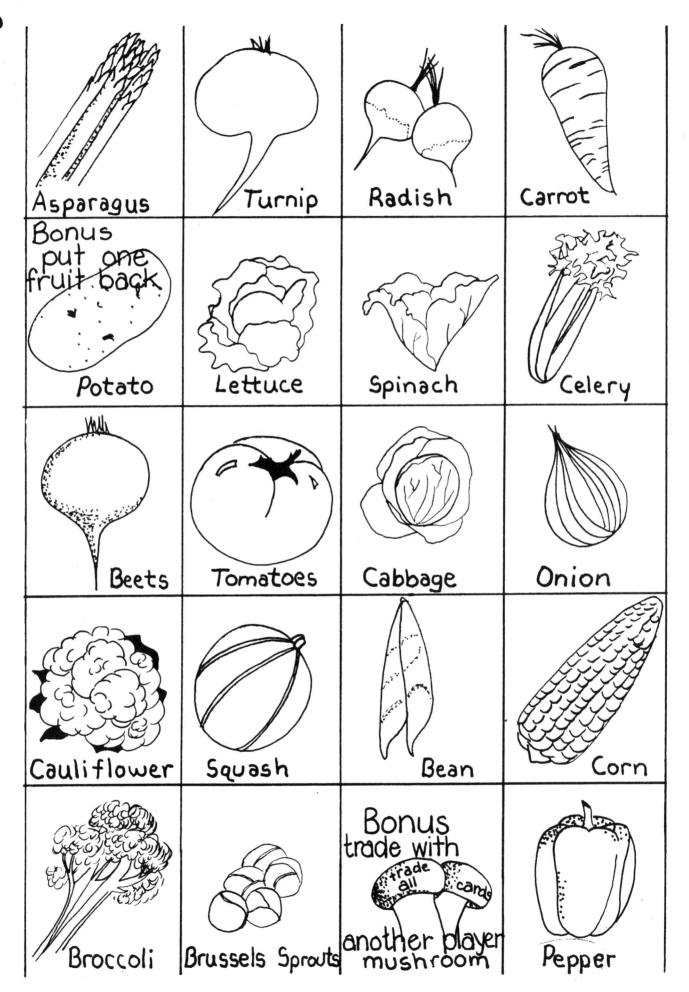

Asparagus	Turnip	Radish	Carrot
Bonus put one fruit back — Potato	Lettuce	Spinach	Celery
Beets	Tomatoes	Cabbage	Onion
Cauliflower	Squash	Bean	Corn
Broccoli	Brussels Sprouts	Bonus trade with another player — mushroom	Pepper